A GIFT FOR

NIKĀḤ

SHAYKH ABDUL RAHEEM LIMBĀDĀ

HAFIZAHULLĀH

Tafseer-Raheemi Publications 2023
info@tafseer-raheemi.com

A Gift for Nikāh
2nd Edition: February 2023 / Sha'bān 1444
ISBN: 978-1-912301-05-8

Author & Editing	*Shaykh* Abdul Raheem Limbādā *Hafizahullāh* (www.tafseer-raheemi.com)
Transcribed by	Maulānā Omer Anwar
Cover Design	*Shaykh* Ahmed *ibn* Maulānā Mohammed Patel
Typesetting	Belal Isakjee
Hadīth Referencing	Maulānā Omer Anwar
Printed by	Elma Basim, Turkey

Other available titles in this series:

A Gift for Ramadhān

Available to purchase from www.tafseer-raheemi.com/shop

CONTENTS

وَجَعَلَ بَيْنَكُم مَّوَدَّةً وَرَحْمَةً ۚ

"And He placed between you Love and Compassion"

Qur'ān 30:21

FOREWORD

In the name of Allāh, the All-Merciful, the Very-Merciful. All praise is for Allāh the Lord of the Worlds; and peace and blessings be upon our master Muhammad, his family, Companions, and all those who follow in their footsteps until the Day of Recompense.

We live in a time where marital conflicts, separations, and divorces are rife. The sheer number of married couples consulting scholars and Imams for arbitration or advice on how to end their marriage makes one wonder if any marriage is actually surviving these days. According to one survey, one in every three or four Muslim marriages is breaking down, and those that do survive do so with their fair share of problems and struggles. Sadly, children – whom Allāh Most High has granted to us as a trust (*amānah*) – suffer the most, with many turning to alcohol, drug-abuse, and other vices as a form of escapism from the troubles at home.

Many factors could be cited for the dire state of marriages, such as not making a sensible and wise choice when selecting a marriage partner, not learning about the guidance provided by Allāh and His Messenger (peace and blessings be upon him) on how to live a married life, not understanding and appreciating the opposite gender, roles of the spouses being mixed up, people entering marriages with high expectations, interference from family and friends, expectations of the in-laws, cultural expectations, porn addiction, obsession with wealth, and people generally having bad character traits and non-reformed hearts.

On the other hand, there is an emerging trend among some young people of not wanting to marry or delaying marriages. Some parents exert undue pressure on their children in terms of financial stability and other aspects before allowing them to marry. Sadly, so many cultural formalities need to be adhered to before a young person can even contemplate marriage – at a time where the temptation to sin is greater than ever and also extremely easy. One should always remember that when the doors of the lawful (*halāl*) are closed, the doors of the unlawful (*harām*) become wide open!

In both scenarios, the institution of marriage – considered an act of worship (*ibādah*) and means of perfecting one's faith (*iman*) – is at risk, at least within some quarters. Allāh Most High has gifted humanity with this beautiful union of man and woman, yet here we are neglectful of its importance and sacredness. The backbone of any good society is a constitution of healthy families produced by sound marital relationships. If marital relations are dire, they affect the children and the community at large.

It is for this reason that the Qur'ān and *Sunnah* emphasise and highlight the importance of marriage and family relations. Maintaining a 'happy' Islamic marriage requires constant nurturing, fostering, and striving. It is not just a case of finding someone suitable, marrying them, and then living happily never after; marriages require much more than that. One must learn about marriage beforehand and then continue to work hard throughout the course of it in order to have a blissful marriage. It is for this very reason that much reward has been promised on marrying and maintaining it in accordance with the spirit of *Shari'a*.

The road towards a healthy and prosperous marriage begins long before one even contemplates marriage. It is imperative to educate oneself on this topic, either by attending marriage courses and workshops or reading books written on marriage.

Sadly, many of us are unaware of even the basics of an Islamic marriage. Often those present at an Islamic marriage ceremony have no idea what the Imam is reciting in Arabic and why he is reciting it. The *Sunnah* of Allāh's Messenger (peace and blessings be upon him) was to recite the three verses of *taqwā* in the marriage sermon in order to remind each party that a marriage cannot be successful without the fear of Allāh and being conscious of the fact that He is watching you, and that you will be answerable for everything you say or do throughout marriage.

There are so many other things to learn about marriage to the point that – I believe – every marriage aspirant should spend a considerable amount of time equipping themselves with necessary knowledge before entering marriage. The Messenger of Allāh (Allāh bless him & grant him peace) said, "The acquisition of knowledge is an obligation upon every Muslim" (*Ibn Mājah*). This refers to seeking knowledge concerning all those matters that affect an individual's everyday life, and as such if one intends to marry it is obligatory to learn about it.

Given this, many scholars – both classical and contemporary – have penned detailed works on this subject in Arabic, Urdu, and other languages. A few books have been penned in English too, but this subject is so vast and multi-dimensional that any new work is welcomed and will contribute positively to what is already available on the subject.

Alhamdulillāh, this book which is in your hands 'A Gift for Nikah' by our dear and respected Shaykh Abdul Raheem Limbada (*Hafizahullāh*) is an invaluable addition to the Muslim bookshelf on the topic of marriage. It is equally beneficial for those seeking to get married, those already married, and those who have children of marriageable age. The book comprehensively and systematically covers the various issues surrounding marriage, from the virtues of marriage, advice on selecting a suitable spouse, to marriage itself and maintaining a healthy marriage once married. It is based on a course which the Shaykh delivered a few years ago in Walsall (UK). May Allāh reward his efforts and the efforts of all those who have assisted him in any way, and may He make this book a means of helping Muslims to uphold healthy Islamic marriages, *Ameen*.

Mufti Muhammad ibn Adam al-Kawtharī *Dāmat Barakātuhum*
Leicester, UK
22/03/2018

FOREWORD

With the Name of Allāh, The Most Merciful, The Very Merciful

I bear witness that there is no god except Allāh ﷻ alone and that Muhammad ﷺ is His servant and Messenger.

This book that you have before you, A Gift for Nikāh is a highly practical and immensely beneficial compilation, authored by our respected teacher. It is a guide, which when read, will surely pave the way towards a blissful marriage for all readers alike.

Marriage culminates a significant aspect of our *deen* and thus having a book like this is much needed for the community at large.

It provides invaluable lessons for those looking to get married and covers an array of issues pertaining to the search process to the engagement period and so on. The unique aspect of this compilation is that it is very practical and takes the reader through all the necessary steps to ensure a blessed marriage.

It addresses common issues that one may face in the search for a potential spouse as well as highlighting and shedding light unto the different dilemmas one may experience. Not only are misconceptions rectified, the book also helps to clarify which actions are purely cultural as opposed to those that are Islamically inspired. Knowing and appreciating the difference is key to ensuring one's marriage is in line with the Sunnah as much as possible.

The systematic and pragmatic nature of this book will, without doubt bring benefit to every reader who is looking to get married as well as for parents and guardians whom are searching for family members.

I benefited thoroughly from this compilation and I pray that Allāh Ta'ālā Grants us the tawfeeq to act upon its messages and lessons.

May Allāh Most High reward the author with the best of rewards, ameen.

Apa Bint Abil Khair *Hafizahāllah*

PREFACE

بِسْمِ اللهِ الرَّحْمٰنِ الرَّحِيْمِ

نحمده ونصلی علی رسوله الکریم۔ اما بعد۔

All praise is for Allāh ﷻ. May the choicest blessings be upon our master and guide Hadhrat Muḥammad Muṣṭafā ﷺ, upon his family members and companions, and upon those who follow them in their footsteps until the Day of Recompense. *Āmīn.*

The book in front of you is in fact the transcription of a course this sinful servant delivered in Masjid Al Farouq, Walsall, UK. The course was organised by my good friends Maulānā Ebrāhīm Esakjee and Maulānā Belal Isakjee. May Allāh ﷻ reward them with the best of rewards in both worlds. *Āmīn.*

Alhamdulillāh, it was attended by approximately 200 people, 120 ladies and 80 gents.

Maulānā Belal requested our good friend Maulānā Omer Anwar to transcribe it. Maulānā Omer not just transcribed it, but also edited it and added references, thereby adding some glitter and gloss to the work. May Allāh ﷻ reward him for his *muḥabbat* with this sinful one. May Allāh ﷻ accept his efforts and be pleased. *Āmīn.*

Nikāḥ is a great *Sunnah* from the *Sunnah* of All the Prophets ﷺ. Allāh ﷻ sent approximately 124,000 Prophets and Messengers to guide humanity. They all entered wedlock except for two; Sayyidunā Īsā and Sayyidunā Yaḥyā ﷺ. Sayyidunā Yaḥyā ﷺ had dedicated his life for worshipping in the *Baytul Maqdis* and he died at a very tender age. Sayyidunā Īsā ﷺ was raised high above the heavens at the age of 33.

It is narrated by Ibn al-Jawzī ﵀ in *Kitāb al-Wafā*, and quoted in *Mishkāt*, that Sayyidunā Īsā ﵇ will come down before the Day of Judgement. He will finish off the Anti-Christ (the *Dajjāl*). He will perform *Ḥajj*, then finally settle down in Madīnah Munawwarah. He will get married and have two sons. He will die in Madīnah Munawwarah and he will be buried beside Rasūlullāh ﷺ.

That leaves only one Prophet from the chain of Prophethood, who didn't enter Wedlock, Sayyidunā Yaḥyā ﵇. Therefore, every Muslim, young or old, should get married with the intention of following the *Sunnah* of all the Prophets, and the *Sunnah* of our own beloved Prophet Muhammad ﷺ who said, '*Nikāḥ* is my *Sunnah*!'

These days we see in the western world that even our own Muslim community looks down upon *nikāḥ*.

Many youngsters say, 'I don't feel like getting married.' Many are content with a life of fornication which is a Major sin. Some youngsters don't want to face the burden of supporting a wife and starting a family. Girls feel comfortable in their parents' home. They don't want the hassle of cooking, cleaning, washing etc. Many want to pursue their careers and achieve high grades. Parents feel happy with the income their daughters are bringing home and are reluctant to lose out. Many don't want to see their daughters moving farther away to a different town or city.

The whole society is in chaos. Then there are so many divorces which lead to many complications; young children being abandoned, single parents, no support, etc.

The purpose of this book is just to portray to our youngsters that marriage is a beautiful concept. Boys and girls should get married at a young age. As soon as the law allows, and as soon as they are mature enough to shoulder the responsibilities.

Girls should not demand huge dowries, separate living facilities, high incomes, fast cars, etc. Simplicity should be adopted. One *Ḥadīth* states, 'Simplicity is part of *Īmān*.' We should hold on to simplicity which is part of *Īmān*.

It is my humble *duā* that Allāh ﷻ accepts this humble effort and makes it beneficial for those who are looking to get married as well as for those who are already married.

May Allāh ﷻ give our community the ability to enjoy life in a *ḥalāl* manner and to avoid all forms of ḥarām actions. *Āmīn.*

Shaykh Abdul Raheem Limbādā *Hafizahullāh*
16 Jamada-al-Ula 1439
2nd February 2018

A COMMAND TO INDIVIDUALS

Allāh ﷻ commands us in the Qur'ān:

فَانْكِحُوْا مَا طَابَ لَكُمْ مِّنَ النِّسَآءِ مَثْنٰى وَثُلٰثَ

وَرُبٰعَ ۚ فَاِنْ خِفْتُمْ اَلَّا تَعْدِلُوْا فَوَاحِدَةً ۝

... Then, marry the women you like, in twos, in threes and in fours. But, if you fear that you will not maintain equity, then [keep to] one woman ...[1]

This is beautiful guidance for marriage. There is permissibility for more than one wife, however the instruction is that if you fear you will not be able to maintain equity between two then you should only marry once. Indeed, Imām Shāfi'ī ﷺ was of the opinion that less is better, meaning that having one spouse is better than having many, as many wives and children could become a burden and distraction from our main purpose in this life, which is to worship and attain Allāh's ﷻ pleasure. However, that being said, there is still permission for more than one.

The word '*fankiḥū*' is a *ḥukm* [command] to every single person who is mature and able to get married to marry, which means we should try to get married as soon as possible and avoid remaining single. Many people in this day and age spend their youth claiming they prefer celibacy and remaining single, pointing to their personal freedom, career, and/or finances as their priority. However, once they reach the age of 35 or 40, they begin to regret this decision and wish they had married earlier, because then it is very difficult to find a spouse. Allāh's ﷻ command here tells us that we should look to marry at a young age, while circumstances are in our favour, as this is the natural way of life, rather than turn away from it then and regret afterwards.

[1] Qur'ān 4:3.

The Companion, Abū Ayyūb 📿 narrates that the Beloved Messenger 📿 stated:

$$\text{أَرْبَعٌ مِنْ سُنَنِ الْمُرْسَلِينَ الْحَيَاءُ وَالتَّعَطُّرُ وَالسِّوَاكُ وَالنِّكَاحُ.}$$

Four [things] are from the Sunan of the Messengers 📿: Al-Ḥayā [Modesty], using Aṭṭar [perfume], the Siwāk [toothbrush stick], and marriage. [2]

Ḥayā, or modesty, was an attribute and characteristic of every single prophet 📿, as was the application of perfume. The Beloved Messenger 📿 would be perfumed by the Mother of the Believers, Lady Ā'ishah 📿 with the best scent available till she could see the sheen of the scent upon his noble head and in his blessed beard.[3] Accordingly, we should also apply perfume and try to have a nice, pleasant smell and appearance, especially when we attend gatherings.

After this the *Siwāk* is mentioned, i.e. to use a toothbrush, toothpaste, or any other product to keep the breath fresh and the mouth clean. As there was no running water during that period, the Mother of the Believers, Lady Ā'ishah 📿 would prepare two bowls of water for the Messenger of Allāh 📿, one for his *Siwāk* [tooth-stick] and one for making *Wudhū'*. Then, whenever Allāh 📿 wished to awaken him from sleep at night, he [📿] would brush his teeth, make *Wudhū*, and perform *Salāh*.[4] In fact, when asked what the first action of the Beloved Messenger 📿 was upon entering the home, the Mother of the Believers, Lady Ā'ishah 📿 replied, '[He would use] the *Siwāk*'.[5] Through eating something, or even through remaining quiet for too long, the mouth can sometimes develop a bad scent, and in order to teach us to be careful in removing this, the Beloved Messenger 📿 imparted this through his emphasis upon this action whenever entering his home. It is an especially good etiquette to make sure the mouth is clean and fresh smelling before approaching your wife to kiss her, otherwise she may feel some discomfort. Moreover, if you

---

[2] Tirmidhī: 1080.
[3] Bukhārī: 5923.
[4] Muslim: 1198; Nasa'ī: 1315.
[5] Muslim: 253a; Nasa'ī: 8; Abū Dāwūd: 51; Ibn Mājah: 305.

drink milk, tea, or coffee, you should take care to rinse your mouth, as milk has a certain amount of fat or greasiness to it which causes the mouth to develop a bad smell.[6]

Finally, the fourth *Sunnah* that is mentioned in the above quoted *Ḥadīth* is marriage. Approximately, 124,000 prophets and messengers were sent by Allāh ﷻ,[7] and all of them married except for two, Yaḥyā ؑ and Īsā ؑ. As for the prophet Īsā ؑ, when he returns to the earth to save the *Ummah* and defeat the *Dajjāl* [Anti-Christ], he will also marry and have two children [8] before dying and being buried alongside the Beloved Messenger ﷺ and his noble companions, Abū Bakr ؓ and Ụmar ؓ.[9] This clearly indicates that marriage is a great *Sunnah* of the prophets, and therefore one should enter wedlock as soon as possible and avoid this habit of remaining single.

A COMMAND TO GUARDIANS

وَاَنْكِحُوا الْاَيَامٰى مِنْكُمْ وَالصّٰلِحِيْنَ مِنْ عِبَادِكُمْ وَاِمَآئِكُمْ ط

اِنْ يَّكُوْنُوْا فُقَرَآءَ يُغْنِهِمُ اللّٰهُ مِنْ فَضْلِهٖ ط وَاللّٰهُ وَاسِعٌ عَلِيْمٌ ○

Arrange the marriage of the spouseless among you, and the capable from among your bondmen and bondwomen. If they are poor, Allāh will enrich them out of His grace. Allāh is All-Encompassing, All-Knowing. [10]

The first order to individuals was '*fankiḥū*' and here the command for guardians is '*wa ankiḥū*', meaning if you are the parent or guardian of a young boy or girl then it is your duty to find a suitable partner for them and get them married. In this day and age, many parents don't fully realise or understand this responsibility, and oft times even when a suitable partner is presented they reject the suitor for flimsy reasons. They must try to understand that Allāh ﷻ has ordered us to arrange for our children's marriages. Consequently, if you are not

[6] Bukhārī: 211, 5609; Muslim: 358 a.

[7] Ibn Ḥibbān: 361; Ibn Ḥātim (Tafsīr): 963.

[8] Kitāb al Fitan (Nuạym bin Ḥammād).

[9] Tirmidhī: 3617.

[10] Qur'ān 24:32.

carrying out this command and are instead rejecting proposals for small, petty reasons, then you are making a big mistake.

Abū Hurairah ﷺ and Abū Ḥātim al-Muzanī ﷺ both narrate that the Messenger of Allāh ﷺ said:

إِذَا خَطَبَ إِلَيْكُمْ مَنْ تَرْضَوْنَ دِينَهُ وَخُلُقَهُ فَزَوِّجُوْهُ
إِلاَّ تَفْعَلُوْا تَكُنْ فِتْنَةٌ فِي الأَرْضِ وَفَسَادٌ عَرِيْضٌ.

"When there comes to you to propose [to someone under your care] one with whose character and religious commitment you are pleased, then marry [her] to him, for if you do not do so, then there will be turmoil [Fitnah] in the land and widespread corruption and discord [Fasād]." [11]

If a person with these two qualities comes to you asking for a hand in marriage, i.e. he is religious minded, follows the *Dīn* [prays *Salāh*, gives *Zakāh*, fasts, recites the Qur'ān, etc.], and has good manners, then immediately accept the proposal and get them married. Do not look at his employment status, bank balance, house, or car, or wait for other things, but rather suffice on these qualities and immediately get them married. This is what '*wa ankiḥū*' entails, that it is upon you to find someone with these qualities and marry your daughter/female relative to him.

Furthermore, if your son or daughter is to present someone to you who meets these two qualities then you should be grateful and, after checking the person's background thoroughly, get them married. Do not become a barrier to your son or daughter's marriage.

ADVICE TO THE YOUTH

Ạbdullāh bin Mas'ūd ﷺ narrates that the Messenger of Allāh ﷺ said:

يَا مَعْشَرَ الشَّبَابِ مَنِ اسْتَطَاعَ مِنْكُمُ الْبَاءَةَ فَلْيَتَزَوَّجْ فَإِنَّهُ أَغَضُّ
لِلْبَصَرِ وَأَحْصَنُ لِلْفَرْجِ وَمَنْ لَمْ يَسْتَطِعْ فَعَلَيْهِ بِالصَّوْمِ فَإِنَّهُ لَهُ وِجَاءٌ.

[11] Tirmidhī: 1084, 1085; Ibn Mājah: 2043.

"O young men, he among you who can afford it, let him get married, for it is most effective in lowering the gaze and guarding chastity; and whoever cannot afford it then he should observe fasting, for it is a means of restraint for him." [12]

There are circumstances where a person does want to marry, but due to a difficult financial situation, or housing situation, or any other similar problem [such as being a fulltime student, etc.] the person is unable to marry. In such circumstances, the Beloved Prophet ﷺ advises us to keep fasts, as continuous fasting for four or five months will help to temporarily reduce a person's sexual urges and compulsions, which will in turn help to protect them. However, the best option available and the number one priority, if you have the ability, is still to get married.

The *Ḥadīth* presents us with two benefits of getting married, which are that it is 'effective in lowering the gaze and guarding chastity'. If you are married and you feel the urge, you can visit your spouse and fulfil your desire, meaning your mind will not be disturbed by nor dwell upon such thoughts as which would normally cloud it if there was no outlet available. Thus, getting married will help you to lower your gaze or look away. One of the primary causes behind addictions to viewing pornography and indecent images is that people are remaining single for longer and so have no outlet for their sexual urges. If they get married, it will help them avoid all these forms of *Zinā* [adultery and fornication], as whenever they feel the need, they can go to their spouse and fulfil their desires. This is the correct way and the way of *Sunnah*.

Jābir bin Ạbdullāh رضي الله عنه narrates that Allāh's Messenger ﷺ said:

إِنَّ الْمَرْأَةَ تُقْبِلُ فِي صُورَةِ شَيْطَانٍ وَتُدْبِرُ فِي صُورَةِ شَيْطَانٍ فَإِذَا أَبْصَرَ أَحَدُكُمُ امْرَأَةً فَلْيَأْتِ أَهْلَهُ فَإِنَّ ذَلِكَ يَرُدُّ مَا فِي نَفْسِهِ و في رواية فَإِنَّ مَعَهَا مِثْلَ الَّذِي مَعَهَا.

[12] Bukhārī: 5065, 5066; Muslim: 1400 a, 1400 c.

Indeed a woman advances and retires in the shape of a devil, so when one of you sees a woman [that he is fascinated by], he should come to his wife, for that will repel what he feels in his heart. And indeed with her [his wife] is the same as that which is with her [the other woman]. [13] [i.e. they both have similar bodies; they are not aliens].

When our gaze falls upon a woman and her appearance seems pleasing to the eye, an occurrence which can happen regardless of how well you protect yourself, and thoughts begin to creep into our minds, the Beloved Prophet ﷺ tells us that we should go to our wives, for they are just as womanly as the one we saw, and this will help protect us. In fact the Beloved Prophet ﷺ imparted this practically when after his gaze accidentally fell upon a woman, he (ﷺ) went to his wife, the Mother of the Believers, Lady Zainab bint Jaḥsh ؓ, who was tanning a leather at the time. He fulfilled his need with her. Later, he ﷺ explained to his companions that this is the way to deal with such circumstances.[14] Hence, the Beloved Prophet ﷺ not only verbally expressed how to deal with this situation but also demonstrated it practically, and this is what is meant by marriage being 'effective in lowering the gaze and guarding chastity'.

It is due to this that it is imperative that our youth marry, and if they cannot do so then they should attempt to control their desires through fasting and other means. They should avoid all such places and devices [television, satellite, the internet, etc.] that can increase the compulsion of their needs and desires. Rather they should spend time in the masjid, or engaged in some work or study or charitable endeavour, so their thoughts can dwell on other things and not be dragged into the fire of passion, lust, and desire.

PROTECTION OF ONE'S FAITH

There is a *Ḥadīth* in which it is stated that:

[13] Muslim: 1403 a; Tirmidhī: 1158; Abū Dāwūd: 2151.

[14] *Ibid.*

مَنْ تَزَوَّجَ فَقَدِ اسْتَكْمَلَ نِصْفَ الإِيمَانِ فَلْيَتَّقِ اللهَ عَزَّ وَجَلَّ فِي النِّصْفِ الْبَاقِي.

Whoever marries has indeed completed half his faith; so let him fear Allāh in the remaining half. [15]

A person has two types of desires: *shahwatul farj* and *shahwatul baṭn*; the desires of his private parts and the desires of his belly. Shaykh Ạbdul Ḥaqq Muḥaddith Dehlavī ﷺ writes in *Lam'āt* [16] that when a person gets married he is protected from *shahwatul farj* and only needs to worry about *shahwatul baṭn*, therefore he should be careful in his earning and whatever he consumes. In this way, he will be protected from both desires and his faith will be complete. This is what is meant by 'so let him fear Allāh in the remaining half'.

Another point to consider is that when the word *niṣf* is used, it does not necessarily mean a literal half but can also mean a great portion, meaning that when a person gets married, a great portion of his faith is completed. Moreover, this can quite easily be understood by observing those unmarried persons who have fallen out of line and are living their lives out of order, misbehaving, clubbing, and falling into *mut'ạh* or *Zinā*, where their *Īmān* is visibly corrupted, diminished, and weak. So, in order to strengthen our *Īmān* and protect it, we get married. Especially so if we are blessed with a good and pious spouse, who will make it fully strong and protected. Many a young man whose behaviour is becoming wretched is married off by his parents to a pious girl and sees his life change for the better. He begins to attend the masjid, he grows his beard and dresses sensibly, and Allāh ﷻ opens his heart to *Īmān*. He may not listen to his mother, but his wife will somehow change him.

اکبر دبے نہیں کسی سلطاں کی فوج سے

---

[15] Bayhaqī (Kitāb Shu'ạbul Īmān); Tabrānī (Awsaṭ); Ḥākim.

[16] Ash'ạtul Lam'āt Sharḥ e Mishkāt.

لیکن شہید ہو گئے بیوی کی نوچ سے [17]

Akbar never suffered a loss to any king's host,
Yet a single exclamation from his wife led to his demise.

Allāh ﷻ has gifted women with this special power through which they can transform a person, either for the better or the worse, depending upon the nature of the woman.

THE MEANING OF NIKĀḤ

Islamically, a *Nikāḥ* is a contract between a male and female wherein they agree to live together in matrimony and fulfil one another's rights. It must include *Ījāb* [proposal] and *qubūl* [acceptance] before two witnesses, and a dowry which is either given straightaway or at an agreed upon later date. According to some *fuqahā* [jurists], the presence of a *Walī* [an advocating guardian for the bride - usually her father] is also a necessity for a *Nikāḥ* to be valid. Others, however, disagree.

For a *Nikāḥ* contract to be considered valid, the *fuqahā* have set some preconditions to ensure its suitability. These are that it should not be made in secrecy, and as a minimum requirement it should be made in the presence of either two male witnesses, or one male and two female witnesses. To perform the *Nikāḥ* in a gathering and to recite the *Khuṭbah* [sermon] of *Nikāḥ* are both *Sunnah* actions, but are not necessary prerequisites for the *Nikāḥ's* validity.

Nikāḥ according to the rules of the *Sharī'ah* is very simple: a proposal and acceptance before two witnesses with the agreement of a dowry. All other rites and rituals around it are either *Sunnah* actions or simply cultural traditions unconnected to Islam [such as *Mehndi*, etc.].

As for the *Sunnah* actions, the Mother of the Believers, Lady Ā'ishah رضي الله عنها narrates that Allāh's Messenger ﷺ said:

[17] Akbar Ilahabādī.

أَعْلِنُوا هَذَا النِّكَاحَ وَاجْعَلُوهُ فِي الْمَسَاجِدِ وَاضْرِبُوا
عَلَيْهِ بِالدُّفُوفِ و في رواية وَاضْرِبُوا عَلَيْهِ بِالْغِرْبَالِ.

Publicise this [rite of] Nikāḥ, and hold it in the Masjids, and beat the 'Duff' [drum-type] for it, [or] and beat the sieve for it. [18]

Therefore a *Nikāḥ* should be announced and publicised, it should be held in a gathering in the masjid, and also the *Khutbah* [sermon] should be read before it is commenced.[19]

PROPHET ĀDAM'S ﷺ NIKĀḤ IN THE HEAVENS

Allāh ﷻ mentions in the Holy Qur'ān:

يٰٓأَيُّهَا النَّاسُ اتَّقُوْا رَبَّكُمُ الَّذِيْ خَلَقَكُمْ مِّنْ نَّفْسٍ وَّاحِدَةٍ وَّخَلَقَ
مِنْهَا زَوْجَهَا وَبَثَّ مِنْهُمَا رِجَالًا كَثِيْرًا وَّنِسَآءً ۚ وَاتَّقُوا اللّٰهَ الَّذِيْ تَسَآءَلُوْنَ
بِهٖ وَالْاَرْحَامَ ۗ اِنَّ اللّٰهَ كَانَ عَلَيْكُمْ رَقِيْبًا ۝

O people, fear your Rabb who created you from a single soul, and from it created its match, and spread many men and women from the two. Fear Allāh in whose name you ask each other [for your rights], and fear [the violation of the rights of] the womb-relations. Surely, Allāh is watchful over you. [20]

When we seek someone's hand in marriage, we ask in the name of Allāh ﷻ, as He is the one who has made this system wherein the man asks for the woman's hand in marriage, and if she accepts then the *Nikāḥ* is done. So we should fear Allāh ﷻ in our daily life and show respect to Him. This verse was recited by the Beloved Prophet ﷺ in the *Nikāḥ* sermon [21] to remind us also that when we marry we must be

---

[18] Tirmidhī: 1089; Ibn Mājah: 1970.

[19] Tirmidhī: 1105; Abū Dāwūd: 2118.

[20] Qur'ān 4:1.

[21] Tirmidhī: 1105; Abū Dāwūd: 2118.

especially careful with regards to the *Ḥuqūq* [rights] of one another's relations. The husband must respect his wife's family; and she must in turn be respectful towards her husband's family. This is what is meant by 'fear [the violation of the rights of] the womb-relations', because 'Allāh ﷻ is watchful over you'.

In the *tafsīr* [exegesis] of this *Āyah* [verse], Ibn Kathīr and others have written that when Ādam ﷺ was in *Jannah* [Paradise] and though he had all the blessings and favours therein, he still felt a deep loneliness and longing. So Allāh ﷻ in His infinite mercy created a companion for him: Ḥawwā ﷺ [Eve]. She was created from the back portion of Ādam's ﷺ left rib while he was sleeping. When Ādam ﷺ woke up, he saw Ḥawwā ﷺ and adored her and had affection for her, and she felt the same towards him.[22] According to *Kitāb at-Taʿbīr*, Ādam ﷺ witnessed the making of Ḥawwā ﷺ in his dream while he slept, seeing her being formed from his top left rib.

Some narrations, attributed to Ibn Ạbbās ؓ, state that Ādam's ﷺ creation was on a Friday in the afternoon. Allāh ﷻ then created for him Ḥawwā ﷺ, his wife, from his left rib while he was asleep. When he woke up and saw her, he felt at ease with her, and he stretched his hand out towards her. The angels said, 'Stop, Ādam.' 'Why?' he asked, 'Didn't Allāh create her for me?' They said, 'Not until you pay her dowry.' 'What is her dowry?' he asked. 'To recite praises thrice upon Muhammad ﷺ.'

Another narration states that when Ādam ﷺ wanted to come close to Ḥawwā ﷺ she requested her *mahr* [dowry]. Ādam ﷺ asked Allāh ﷻ as to what he should give her. Allāh ﷻ replied, 'Send twenty *Durūd* [salutations] on my chosen slave Muḥammad bin 'Ạbdullāh ﷺ. So Ādam ﷺ did so.[23] Shaykh Ạbdul Ḥaqq Muḥaddith Dehlavī ؒ has also reported this second narration in *Jazbul Qulūb ilā Diyāril Maḥbūb*, as has Hadhrat Shaykh Muḥammad Zakarīyyā ؒ in the seminal *Fazāil-e-Durūd Sharīf.*

[22] Tafsīr Ibn Kathīr.

[23] Al Qawlul Badī': p.132.

These narrations also help us to understand the meaning of the verse:

هُوَ الَّذِيْ خَلَقَكُمْ مِّنْ نَّفْسٍ وَّاحِدَةٍ وَّجَعَلَ مِنْهَا زَوْجَهَا لِيَسْكُنَ اِلَيْهَا ۝

He is the One who has created you from a single soul, and out of him created his wife, so that he may find comfort in her. [24]

A husband and wife attain *sukūn* [serenity] and comfort from one another and in each other, which is why when we get married we feel good in each other's presence. And this feeling of *sukūn* and companionship is one that should be nurtured, so that the feeling of calmness and serenity continues to grow. A husband and wife should become inseparable, especially in the early stages of marriage when they should briefly put all other friendships aside and spend lots of time with one another, becoming each other's best friends.

Some of the lessons we learn from the marriage of Ādam ﷺ and his wife, Ḥawwā ﷺ, are that: firstly, in the sight of Allāh ﷻ, the natural and intended form of marriage is between a man and woman, rather than between people of the same gender. Secondly, the natural and intended form of a relationship between a man and a woman is through *Nikāḥ* rather than just cohabitation.

Finally, marriage is akin to a mutually agreed contract. For example, if two people were to go into business together, there is a chance that there may be misunderstanding, miscommunication, or disagreement which leads to the breaking down of the business partnership, which could all be avoided if the roles, responsibilities, and rights were agreed upon and drawn up in a contract between the two and written beforehand, so no one can back out. This provides a certain amount of reassurance and security for each partner, allowing them to undertake the joint venture with confidence. Similarly, when two people marry, the *Nikāḥ* is a contract and agreement that they will stay with one another and fulfil each other's rights, and this contract is what makes them *ḥalāl* for one another.

---

[24] Qur'ān 7:189.

THE IMPORTANCE AND PURPOSE OF MARRIAGE

Firstly, we should get married because it is the *ḥukm* [command] of our Rabb, Allāh ﷻ. Secondly, we should get married because it is the *Sunnah* of the Beloved Prophet ﷺ, and the *Sunnah* of all Allāh's ﷻ prophets. If we marry with this intention, that we are acting upon Allāh's ﷻ command and following the *Sunnah* of the Beloved Prophet ﷺ, then the *Nikāḥ* becomes a means of reward. Whether you make this intention or not the marriage will take place, but if this intention is made then it becomes a means of continuous reward.

Regarding intention in *Nikāḥ*, I was once with Shaykh Yūnus رحمه الله in South Africa in 2000 CE, where the Shaykh conducted a *Nikāḥ*. Before the *Nikāḥ* he addressed the gathering and said, 'Brothers, before every act of worship we must make an intention, such as when we pray the *Zuhr ṣalāh* we must make the intention of praying four *rak'ah* of *Zuhr* for the sake of Allāh ﷻ, otherwise the *ṣalāh* will not be valid. *Nikāḥ* is also an act of worship and also requires intention: the intention that you are entering into *Nikāḥ* to follow the *Sunnah*, that you are entering into *Nikāḥ* to protect your modesty and chastity, and that you are entering into *Nikāḥ* to increase your progeny and to accept whatever gift Allāh ﷻ bestows upon you in this regard.'

SAFEGUARDING ONE'S YOUTH [PHYSICALLY & SPIRITUALLY]

It is important to marry because it safeguards and protects us from *Zinā* and fornication, and from falling into many other vices such as masturbation, pornography, homosexuality, etc. Marriage provides a solution to the tensions that arise through sexual desires, whereas when you remain single, it becomes easy to fall into bad habits.

Regarding the subject of masturbation, whether male or female, Imām Mālik رحمه الله has deemed it to be *ḥarām*, citing the following verses as a proof of this:

وَالَّذِيْنَ هُمْ لِفُرُوْجِهِمْ حٰفِظُوْنَ ○ اِلَّا عَلٰٓى اَزْوَاجِهِمْ اَوْ مَا مَلَكَتْ اَيْمَانُهُمْ
فَاِنَّهُمْ غَيْرُ مَلُوْمِيْنَ ○ فَمَنِ ابْتَغٰى وَرَآءَ ذٰلِكَ فَاُولٰٓئِكَ هُمُ الْعٰدُوْنَ ○

[Success is really attained by the believers] "Who guard their private parts except from their wives or from those [bondwomen who are] owned by their hands, as they are not to be blamed. However, those who seek sexual pleasure beyond that are the transgressors." [25]

According to Imām Mālik ﵀, masturbation falls under 'those who seek beyond that'. They cross the line beyond what Allāh ﷻ has allowed, which is to only take sexual pleasure from your wives or [in previous times] concubines. [26] Regarding the *Ḥanafī* opinion, Kamāluddīn bin al-Humām (d. 861 AH/1457 CE) writes in *Fatḥ al-Qadīr* [27] that it is *makrūh taḥrīmī*, severely disliked and very close to being *ḥarām*, but cannot be regarded as being explicitly *ḥarām* as there is no definitive evidence for this within the Qur'ān and *Ḥadīth*. Instead it is severely disliked because of the repercussions of its practice and may be regarded as a lesser sin due to them, but not definitively *ḥarām* as is the case with *Zinā*. A major difference between fornication and masturbation is that the former involves two people and its consequences could harm still more, whereas with masturbation the person is alone and only harms himself. Due to these reasons, the *Ḥanafī* School holds the position that masturbation is *makrūh taḥrīmī* but not *ḥarām*.

Imām Aḥmad bin Ḥanbal ﵀ does not regard it as *ḥarām*, according to Ibn Qudāmah al-Maqdisī ﵀ in *Al-Mughnī*. However, there are also two other opinions attributed to Imām Aḥmad ﵀: the first that it is *ḥarām*; the second that it is a *makrūh* [disliked] but permissible action only at a time of extreme need. [28]

Furthermore, *Nikāḥ* is also important for the purpose of procreation and protecting ones lineage and pedigree. This is

---

[25] Qur'ān 23: 5-7.

[26] Tafsīr Qurtubī 15: 11-12.

[27] The commentary on *Al-Hidāyah* and not Imām Shawkānī's *Tafsīr*.

[28] Ibn Rajab's Al-Qawā'iḍ: 246.

something the modern youth rarely take into consideration. If you have children they will give *ṣadaqah* on your behalf and pray for you after your demise. Abū Hurairah ﷺ narrates that the Messenger of Allāh ﷺ said:

إِنَّ الرَّجُلَ لَتُرْفَعُ دَرَجَتُهُ فِي الْجَنَّةِ فَيَقُولُ
أَنَّى هَذَا فَيُقَالُ بِاسْتِغْفَارِ وَلَدِكَ لَكَ.

A man will be raised in status in Paradise and will ask, 'Where did this come from?' And it will be said, 'From your son's prayers for your forgiveness.' [29]

Therefore, if we have children, they can be of benefit to us in this world and the next, *Inshāllāh. Nikāḥ* will help to protect our lineage so we can have children who survive us and carry on our line, and add to our book of good deeds long after we are gone. This is why our elders and the previous generations would try to have many children, whereas the current trend is for couples to only have two children. Having lots of children is something which is desired in *Sharī'ah*, so the children can become a means of forgiveness for their parents.

A *ṣaḥābī* by the name of Ạkkāf bin Wadā'ạ al-Hilālī ﷺ came to the Messenger of Allāh ﷺ one day. The Messenger of Allāh ﷺ asked him, 'O Ạkkāf! Do you have a wife?' He replied, 'No.' 'A concubine?' 'No.' 'And you are well-to-do?' 'Yes, *Alhamdulillāh*.' The Beloved Prophet ﷺ then said, 'Then you are akin to the devil's brethren! If you want to be like the Christian monks, then you are of them. And if you are from us, then do as we do for indeed *Nikāḥ* is from our *Sunnah*. The Beloved Prophet ﷺ further admonished, 'Woe to you, Ạkkāf! Marry, because now you are counted among the sinners.' Upon this, Ạkkāf bin Wadā'ạ al-Hilālī ﷺ requested the Beloved Prophet ﷺ to marry him to whomever he wished, and so the Messenger of Allāh ﷺ married him to Karīma bint Kulthūm al-Ḥimyarī. [30] The Beloved Prophet ﷺ has also stated in another narration that:

[29] Ibn Mājah: 3660; Musnad Aḥmad: 10618.

[30] Muṣannaf Ạbd Al-Razzāq; Musnad Aḥmad; Tabrānī: 14599.

وَمَا فِي الْجَنَّةِ أَعْزَبُ.

There will be none without a wife in Paradise. [31]

Subsequently, if one wishes to live a heavenly life upon this earth, the logical conclusion is that he and she should marry. Moreover, we can also surmise from this that marriage and married life should be a pleasurable, enjoyable experience and something to look forward to. Certain people make jests about husbands and wives and married life, which is something I strongly dislike as this type of humour and joking tends to put off people from marrying. Besides this, to make fun of married life is, in a certain sense, to make fun of the *Sunnah* and should be avoided. Similarly, if you receive a message over social media joking about such matters, you should ignore it and not forward it on to other people, because you may inadvertently then become the cause of putting someone off marrying.

In *Sahīh al-Bukhārī* there is the following narration:

عَنْ سَعِيدِ بْنِ جُبَيْرٍ، قَالَ قَالَ لِي ابْنُ عَبَّاسٍ هَلْ تَزَوَّجْتَ
قُلْتُ لاَ. قَالَ فَتَزَوَّجْ فَإِنَّ خَيْرَ هَذِهِ الأُمَّةِ أَكْثَرُهَا نِسَاءً.

Sa'īd bin Jubair narrates that, 'Ibn Ạbbās asked me, "Are you married?" I replied, "No." He said, "Marry, for the best person of this Ummah [i.e. the Beloved Messenger ﷺ] had the largest number of wives."' [32]

The Messenger of Allāh, the Noble Prophet Muḥammad ﷺ was not just the best of this *Ummah*, but the best of all mankind and the best of all of Allāh's creation. He ﷺ had eleven wives, two of whom died during his lifetime and nine who lived on after his passing. If marriage were something reprehensible, unscrupulous, or unbecoming then the Beloved Messenger ﷺ would not have married. Rather it is good and virtuous and through this our *Dīn* became complete, because we have every aspect of life covered in the *Sunnah*, unlike the Christians for whom there is no primary example of marriage from which to take

[31] Muslim: 2834 a.

[32] Bukhārī: 5069.

their rulings, as the prophet Īsā ﷺ did not marry during his initial period of life upon the earth. In Islam, everything is covered and there are rulings available for every aspect of marriage, from proposal, dowry, and *Nikāḥ* to procreation and cleanliness thereafter.

WHEN DOES NIKĀḤ BECOME FARDH[OBLIGATORY]?

There are certain circumstances in which *Nikāḥ* becomes *Fardh*. If a person is young, healthy, and has the means to marry and his sexual urges are beyond his control, meaning he is fornicating or is at risk of falling into fornication, then *Nikāḥ* becomes *Fardh* upon him. Since *Zinā* is *ḥarām*, then the opposite becomes *Fardh*.

WHEN DOES NIKĀḤ BECOME WĀJIB [NECESSARY]?

In *Kanz al-Daqāiq* it is stated regarding *Nikāḥ* that:

وَهُوَ سُنَّةٌ وَ عِنْدَ التَّوَقَانِ وَاجِبٌ.

It is Sunnah but under intense desire it becomes wājib. [33]

This is in the case when one is not fornicating or at risk of fornication, but you have the means to marry as well as the urge and desire. The need is there and the means are there, but you have not fallen into wrongdoing. And so, to protect yourself, it becomes *wājib* to marry. *Wājib* is one degree below *Fardh* in necessity.

WHEN DOES NIKĀḤ BECOME SUNNAH [EMPHASISED SUNNAH]?

Nikāḥ is *Sunnah* under all normal circumstances. As Ạbdullāh bin Mas'ūd ﷺ is famously reported to have said, 'If I had ten days left to

[33] *Kanz al-Daqāiq*: p.116.

live, and I knew I would die by the end of them, and I had enough time to get married, I would get married for fear of *fitnah* [temptation].'[34] An eminent and pious *ṣaḥābī* is worried that his ego or desire could lead him into sin, even over such a short period. It makes sense then for all of us, who have nowhere near the equivalent piety or *taqwā*, to marry and protect ourselves from falling into such danger.

Abū Muslim al-Khawlānī (d. 65 AH/684 CE) ﷺ would address the elders amongst his community and say to them, 'Marry off your children who have come of age, for if you do not, their desires will intensify. And desires have no ears by which to hear sound judgement or wisdom.' This is especially so in this day and age, when access to all sorts of media spurs the youth towards undesirable actions, so we should marry them off as soon as possible.

WHEN DOES NIKĀḤ BECOME MAKRŪH TAḤRĪMĪ [PROHIBITIVELY DISLIKED]?

When a person is unable to fulfil marital rights, or is a very angry and aggressive person, and is at risk of committing *Zulm* [injustice and oppression] towards a spouse then *Nikāḥ* is *makrūh*. Similarly, if he already has one wife and desires to marry a second, but will be incapable of being just and fair towards them and will lean towards one or the other, then this second *Nikāḥ* is *makrūh*. Again, if he has only enough money to support one wife, then a second *Nikāḥ* is *makrūh*.

WHEN DOES NIKĀḤ BECOME HARĀM [UNLAWFUL]?

If a man is a eunuch, unable to perform the primary responsibility of a husband, it is *Ḥarām* for him to marry. Similarly, if someone is insane then they should not get married either. Also, if a person has a deadly transmittable disease such as HIV, then it is *Ḥarām* for them to marry, because they will put the other person's life at risk.

[34] Sunan Sa'īd bin Manṣūr: 493.

THE RESPONSIBILITY OF PARENTS IN GETTING THEIR CHILDREN MARRIED

The responsibility of parents to find suitable partners for their sons and daughters has already been discussed. However, it is pertinent to mention here that it is not only for the boy's parents to actively search and send proposals for marriage. If a girl's parents find a boy who is a good match for their daughter, then they should send a proposal to that family. It is only the custom of the people from the Asian culture that dictates that only the boy's side should propose. We can find examples of the opposite in the lives of the *Sahābāh* ﷺ.

Lady Ḥafsah bint Ụmar ﷺ became a widow upon the death of her husband, Khunais bin Ḥudhāfah As-Sahmī ﷺ. He had been one of the Companions of the Prophet ﷺ who fought in the Battle of Badr, and he died in Al-Madīnah. After his death, Ụmar ﷺ narrates that:

فَلَقِيتُ عُثْمَانَ بْنَ عَفَّانَ ؓ فَعَرَضْتُ عَلَيْهِ حَفْصَةَ فَقُلْتُ إِنْ شِئْتَ أَنْكَحْتُكَ حَفْصَةَ . فَقَالَ سَأَنْظُرُ فِي ذَلِكَ . فَلَبِثْتُ لَيَالِيَ فَلَقِيتُهُ فَقَالَ مَا أُرِيدُ أَنْ أَتَزَوَّجَ يَوْمِي هَذَا . قَالَ عُمَرُ ؓ فَلَقِيتُ أَبَا بَكْرٍ الصِّدِّيقَ ؓ فَقُلْتُ إِنْ شِئْتَ أَنْكَحْتُكَ حَفْصَةَ فَلَمْ يَرْجِعْ إِلَيَّ شَيْئًا فَكُنْتُ عَلَيْهِ أَوْجَدَ مِنِّي عَلَى عُثْمَانَ ؓ فَلَبِثْتُ لَيَالِيَ فَخَطَبَهَا إِلَيَّ رَسُولُ اللهِ ﷺ فَأَنْكَحْتُهَا إِيَّاهُ فَلَقِيَنِي أَبُو بَكْرٍ ؓ فَقَالَ لَعَلَّكَ وَجَدْتَ عَلَيَّ حِينَ عَرَضْتَ عَلَيَّ حَفْصَةَ فَلَمْ أَرْجِعْ إِلَيْكَ شَيْئًا . قُلْتُ نَعَمْ . قَالَ فَإِنَّهُ لَمْ يَمْنَعْنِي حِينَ عَرَضْتَ عَلَيَّ أَنْ أَرْجِعَ إِلَيْكَ شَيْئًا إِلاَّ أَنِّي سَمِعْتُ رَسُولَ اللهِ ﷺ يَذْكُرُهَا وَلَمْ أَكُنْ لأُفْشِيَ سِرَّ رَسُولِ اللهِ ﷺ وَلَوْ تَرَكَهَا نَكَحْتُهَا .

I went to Ụthmān bin Ạffān ﷺ and offered Ḥafsah ﷺ in marriage to him. I said, 'If you wish, I will marry you to Ḥafsah.' He replied, 'I will think on it.' A few days passed, then I met him and he said, 'It seems that I do not want to get married at the moment.'

Then I met Abū Bakr As-Ṣiddīq 🌺 *and said: 'If you wish, I will marry Ḥafsah to you.' Abū Bakr* 🌺 *remained silent and did not give me any answer, and I felt more upset with him than I had with Uthmān* 🌺. *Several days passed, and then the Messenger of Allāh* 🌺 *proposed marriage to her and I married her to him. Abū Bakr* 🌺 *met me and said, 'Perhaps you felt upset with me when you offered Ḥafsah in marriage to me, and I did not give you any answer?' I said, 'Yes.' He said, 'Nothing prevented me from giving you an answer when you made the offer to me, except the fact that I had heard the Messenger of Allāh* 🌺 *speak of her, and I did not want to disclose the secret of the Messenger of Allāh* 🌺. *If he had left her, then I would have married her.'* [35]

This ḥadīth proves that if the parents of a girl know of a suitable match for her, they can take the initiative and approach the family of the boy. Similarly, if a girl's parent approaches and offers her hand in marriage, the boy's family should not consider this as something scandalous or immoral.

WHAT AGE IS A PERSON READY FOR MARRIAGE?

Sometimes some of our Islamic guidance is on one side and the law of the land is on the other side, with some contradiction between the two. At such times, it is important to try to keep both things in consideration and ensure the law of the land is not broken. The legal minimum age to enter into a marriage in the UK is sixteen years, although this requires parental consent if a participant is under eighteen in England and Wales. We should abide by the law of the land.

Islamically, *Nikāḥ* can be performed as soon as a person is *bāligh*, i.e. has reached the age of puberty. This also explains the marriage of the Mother of the Believers, Lady Ā'ishah 🌺. We will narrate here the ḥadīth regarding her *nikāḥ* with Rasūlullāh 🌺.

After Lady Khadījah 🌺 passed away, Khawlah bint Ḥakīm 🌺 came [to the Messenger of Allāh 🌺] and asked, 'Will you not marry, O

---

[35] Nasa'ī: 3248, 3259.

Prophet of Allāh ﷺ?' He ﷺ said, 'To whom?' She said, 'If you like, a virgin, or a previously married woman.' He ﷺ asked, 'Who is the virgin?' She said, 'The daughter of the most beloved of Allāh's creation to you, Ā'ishah bint Abū Bakr ◉.' He ﷺ asked, 'And who is the previously married?' She replied, 'Sawdah bint Zam'a ◉; she believed in you and has followed you in what you say.' He ﷺ said, 'So go, and mention me to them.'

So she entered Abū Bakr's ◉ house and said, 'O Um Rūmān, what great good and blessing did Allāh grant you!' She asked, 'And what is that?' She said, 'The Prophet ﷺ sent me to propose his marriage to Ā'ishah ◉.' She said, 'Wait for Abū Bakr ◉ to come.' Abū Bakr ◉ came and she said, 'O Abū Bakr, what great good and blessings did Allāh grant you!' He asked, 'And what is that?' She said, 'The Prophet ﷺ sent me to propose his marriage to Ā'ishah ◉.' He said: 'Is she good for him? She is his brother's daughter.'

She returned to the Prophet ﷺ and mentioned that to him. He ﷺ said, 'Return and tell him I am your brother and you are my brother in Islam, and your daughter is good for me.'

She returned and mentioned that to him. He said: 'Wait.' And he went out. Um Rūmān said that Mut'im bin Adīyy had proposed for her to his son, and by Allāh, Abū Bakr never made a promise and broke it.

Abū Bakr ◉ went to Mut'im while his wife, the mother of the potential-groom, was with him, She said, 'O son of Abu Quhāfah, perhaps if we marry our son to your daughter you will bring him into the religion which you practice.' He turned to her husband Mut'im and said, 'What is she saying?' He replied, 'She says what you have heard.'

Abū Bakr ◉ left, [realising that] Allāh had [just] removed the problem he had in his mind about his promise. He returned and told Khawlah: 'Invite the Prophet ﷺ to come over.' She invited him, and he married him to her, while Lady Ā'ishah ◉ was six years old then.[36]

The Mother of the Believers, Lady Ā'ishah ◉ herself narrates, 'The Prophet ﷺ engaged me when I was a girl of six. We went to Madīnah and stayed at the home of the Banī al Hārith bin Khazraj. Then I got ill

---

[36] Musnad Ahmad: 25241, 25810.

and my hair fell off. Later on my hair grew [again] and my mother, Um Rūmān, came to me while I was playing on a swing with some of my friends. She called me, and I went to her, not knowing what she wanted to do to me. She caught me by the hand and made me stand at the door of the house. I was breathless then, and when my breathing became alright, she took some water and rubbed my face and head with it. Then she took me into the house. There in the house I saw some Anṣārī women who said, "Best wishes and Allāh's Blessing and good luck." Then she entrusted me to them and they prepared me [for the marriage]. Unexpectedly Allāh's Apostle ﷺ came to me in the forenoon and my mother handed me over to him, and at that time I was a girl of nine years of age [i.e. close to ten]. [37]

From this account we can take a few points. Firstly, the Messenger of Allāh ﷺ did not propose himself, but rather it was Khawlah bint Ḥakīm ﵂ who went on his behalf and who suggested the marriage in the first place. Secondly, Lady Ā'ishah ﵂, though six years of age, was already engaged at the time of the proposal. This all shows that the norms of society at that time were much different to those of the current age, and such engagements and proposals were normal aspects of society. Moreover, the Messenger of Allāh ﷺ did not bring her into his house, the consummation of the marriage did not occur until it was urged by the bride's father, Abū Bakr ﵁. The Mother of the Believers, Lady Ā'ishah ﵂ narrates that when she migrated to Madīnah, she dwelt among the family of her father, Abū Bakr ﵁. Until Abū Bakr ﵁ himself went to the Messenger of Allāh ﷺ and queried:

مَا يَمْنَعُكَ أَنْ تَبْنِيَ بِأَهْلِكَ؟

'What prevents you from consummating with your wife?' [38]

The Beloved Prophet ﷺ had no property at which to keep her, so Abū Bakr ﵁ himself bought a small property adjacent to the *masjid* for them to stay in and sent Lady Ā'ishah ﵂ to live there. This occurred

---

[37] Bukhārī: 3894; Muslim: 1422 a.

[38] Fatḥul Bārī: vol.7: p.225; Mustadrak Ḥākim: vol.4: p.85; Tabaqāt Ibn S'ạd: Vol.1: p.206.

after the *Hijrah* [emigration to Madīnah] which was three years after the marriage took place, when Lady Ā'ishah ﵂ was nearly ten. This confirms that both her parents felt she had matured and was well into puberty, and Lady Ā'ishah ﵂ herself states:

إِذَا بَلَغَتِ الْجَارِيَةُ تِسْعَ سِنِينَ فَهِيَ امْرَأَةٌ.

When a girl reaches nine years of age, then she is a woman. [39]

This attests to the fact that Lady Ā'ishah ﵂ observed that she and girls her age were physically and mentally mature by that age. Lady Ā'ishah ﵂ then had indeed matured well physically [40], as the family of Abū Bakr ﵁ were affluent and could provide the nutrition and provision for her to do so. Lady Ā'ishah ﵂ narrates, 'My mother intended to make me gain weight to send me to the [house of] the Messenger of Allah [ﷺ]. But nothing which she desired benefited me till she gave me cucumber with fresh dates to eat. Then I gained as much weight [as she desired]. '[41] Accordingly, in Islamic law, as soon as a boy or girl enters into puberty and physically mature enough to have sexual relations, then their *Nikāḥ* is permissible.

There are many other similar examples from that period of time of marriage at the age of puberty. Ạbdullāh bin Ạmr bin Ạāṣ ﵄ was only 11 years younger than his father Ạmr bin Ạāṣ ﵁, i.e. Ạmr bin Ạāṣ ﵁ married early at or before the age of 12.[42] Imām Shāfi'ī ﵀ states that, 'In Sana'ā, I saw a grandmother who was [just] twenty one years of age. She had reached puberty at age nine and given birth at ten; her daughter also reached puberty at nine and then [also] gave birth aged ten.' [43] One of the narrators of *Ṣaḥīḥ al-Bukhārī*. Ḥasan bin Ṣāliḥ ﵁, also reports that, 'I observed a neighbour of ours who had become a

[39] Tirmidhī: 1109; Ạwn al-Mạ'būd: 2093.

[40] Dāwūdī cited in Sharḥ Muslim of Nawawī: Vol.9: p.207.

[41] Abū Dāwūd: 3903.

[42] al-Tārīkh Al Kabīr of Bukhārī: Vol.5: p.5; Siyar Ạ'lām an-Nubalā: Vol.3: p.80; al-Iṣābah fī Tamyīz al-Ṣaḥābah; al-Jawāhir al-lu'luwīyya.

[43] Bayhaqī (Sunan al-Kubrā): 1531.

grandmother at twenty-one years of age.'[44] Consequently, it is evident that these people lived in a dissimilar society and dealt with everything differently, and it is both illogical and imbalanced to judge them according to today's norms.

Having said this, even in this day and age, cultures across the globe differ and a diversity of societal norms exist even now. The age of consent or marriage in countries across Africa [age 12 in Angola, 13 in Burkina Faso, Comoros, and Niger], Asia [9 in Afghanistan, 12 in the Philippines, 13 in Japan and South Korea, 14 in China], the Americas [13 in Argentina, 14 in Brazil], and even Europe [age 14 in Germany, Italy, Portugal, etc.] are still based at or near the age of puberty. Historically, child marriages were common into the late 19th Century in the UK, with age of consent in England within the range of 10 to 12 until 1875.[45] In the United States, the age of consent was set at 10 or 12 in most states, with the exception of Delaware where it was 7, right up until the 20th Century.[46] Among the United States' Mormonist sects, polygamist marriages with girls as young as 12 have been happening to this day and age.[47]

In conclusion, we can see that the Islamic view for the age of consent/marriage to coincide with the signs of puberty, such as menstruation or pubic hair, and enough physical maturity to have sexual relations has been the commonly held view and the rule rather than the exception, both globally and throughout history. According to the *Sharī'ah*, a girl comes of age through either menstruation, nocturnal emission, or sexual intercourse; a boy comes of age through either nocturnal emission or sexual intercourse. And if none of these occur, then in both cases at the age of 15 according to the lunar calendar, or 14 years and 7 months according to the solar calendar, they will be considered as having reached maturity.

Once they are of age and legally old enough to marry, then their marriage should be arranged as quick as possible as this is the best

---

[44] Ibid.

[45] Robertson, S. (2013) "Age of Consent Laws," in *Children and Youth in History* (online).

[46] Ibid.

[47] Pilkington, E. (2011) "Fundamentalist Sect Leader Jailed for Life for Sex with Child Brides." *The Guardian*.

course of action. Likewise, once they are married they should begin living as husband and wife straightaway and no delay should be made in sending the bride to the groom's house. This is a recent phenomenon, where couples are married and continue to live separately for various reasons for anywhere up to a year, and only keep contact through phone calls and social media. This can be dangerous, as if there is an argument, misunderstanding, or miscommunication in this long-distance contact, there could be disastrous consequences for their relationship, and could possibly lead to divorce. There have been many such cases. On the other hand, if they are living together as husband and wife, perhaps even have children, then their relationship is being strengthened on a daily basis and any such incidents are usually diffused within a day or so.

In addition, to delay the sending of the bride to live with her husband is against the *Sunnah*, as the Beloved Prophet ﷺ married eleven times and his wives came to live with him the very evening of the *Nikāḥ*, with the exception of Lady Ā'ishah ﵂ whose departure to the Beloved Prophet's ﷺ house was delayed until the age of maturity.

WHAT SHOULD ONE LOOK FOR WHEN CHOOSING AN IDEAL SPOUSE?

Abū Huraira ﵁ narrates that the Prophet ﷺ said:

تُنْكَحُ الْمَرْأَةُ لأَرْبَعٍ لِمَالِهَا وَلِحَسَبِهَا وَجَمَالِهَا

وَلِدِينِهَا فَاظْفَرْ بِذَاتِ الدِّينِ تَرِبَتْ يَدَاكَ .

A woman may be married for four reasons: for her wealth, her status, her beauty, and her religion. So you should marry the religious woman [otherwise] you will be ruined.[48]

This does not mean that the other three factors should be taken completely out of consideration, however, the main priority should be a person's religious inclination. There was a man once who was

[48] Bukhārī: 5090; Muslim 1466.

seeking a potential match for his daughter. It so happened that he was in possession of a very wise and intelligent slave whose advice he sought in this matter. The slave said, 'The Jewish people look towards the wealth of a man, and give their daughters' hands to the one with the most wealth, thinking he will be able to keep her in luxury and comfort. As for the Christians, they look towards beauty and prefer the most handsome and beautiful person to marry them. The noble Arab tribe of the *Quraysh* looked towards status and would only marry their daughters into a house of equal stature. But Islam teaches us that we should look towards piety and religiousness. If you find someone who is pious and God-fearing, you should give your daughter's hand to him.' Upon hearing this, the man announced that he had freed his slave, and gave his daughter's hand to him as there was no one more pious or God-fearing than him.

Shaykh Aḥmed Ạlī Lāhorī's daughter had reached the age of marriage and had received many proposals, but the Shaykh refrained from accepting any as he sought someone of high religious character and piety. As was his habit, he entered the masjid at the time of *Tahajjud* to perform his nightly prayers and came upon a student who was busy in his own *ṣalāh*. The Shaykh recognised him as one who was a constant attendee of *dhikr* gatherings and one who frequents the masjid. The Shaykh approached him and asked him whether he would like to marry, upon which the student replied, 'Who would give their daughter to such as him, as he was very poor.' Shaykh Aḥmed Ạlī Lāhorī gave his own daughter in marriage to him.

Sa'īd bin al-Musayyib ﵀ is a famous *tābiʻī* who was married to the daughter of Abu Hurairah ﵁. He is renowned as one of 'The Seven *Fuqahā* of Madīnah', and the most eminent of them.[49] After Ạbd al-Malik bin Marwān had taken the caliphate and command over Madīnah, he requested Sa'īd bin al-Musayyib ﵀ that he marry his daughter [born from his marriage to Abu Hurairah's ﵁ daughter] to the prince, al-Walīd, when the latter was announced as the heir apparent, but Sa'īd bin al-Musayyib ﵀ refused and was not willing to budge from this stance despite the Caliph's insistence. Until Ạbd al-

[49] Ibn Sa'd (*Tabaqāt* Vol.5 trans. as Aisha Bewley, *The Men of Madīnah* Vol. 2: p.81).

Malik bin Marwān had had enough and ordered for him to be whipped one hundred times on a cold day, and had a pitcher of water poured over him and made him a wear a robe of wool. Sa'īd bin al-Musayyib's stance arose from his desire to marry his daughter to a god-fearing man.

Ạbdullāh bin Abī Wadā'ạ narrates that: 'I used to sit in the gatherings of Sa'īd bin al-Musayyib. I was absent for some days and when I went back, he asked me, "Where have you been?" '"My wife died and that made me to be busy," I replied. 'He said, "Why didn't you tell us so that we could have witnessed the burial." Then, when I intended to rise [and take my leave], he asked, "Have you taken another woman [i.e. wife]?" '"May Allāh Almighty have mercy on you," I said, "Who would marry their daughter to me while, other than two or three dirham, I possess nothing?" '"I shall," He said. '"Will you do this?" I asked [incredulous]. '"O yes," he replied. Then he began to praise Allāh Almighty, said benediction upon the Prophet ﷺ and married her to me with my two or three dirham. I stood up and did not know what to do out of extreme joy. I went back to my house then I began to think of whom I could take and borrow things from. I observed the Maghrib prayer and headed back to my house to rest. I was alone and fasting and my supper – made of bread and stew – was brought to break my fast, when all of a sudden, I heard knocking at the door.

'I enquired who it was and the reply came, "Sa'īd." My mind went through all the people by the name of "Sa'īd" – except for Sa'īd bin al-Musayyib himself, as he was not seen for 40 years except, that he was in his house or the Masjid! I went out to meet the person and suddenly I found Sa'īd bin al-Musayyib standing there. The thought came to me that perhaps he came to announce a change of heart – that he would not give me his daughter.

'"O Abū Muḥammad," I said, "why didn't you send for me? If you had, I would have answered you." '"Never. You have more right to be visited." '"What would you have of me?" I asked. 'He replied, "You were once with no wife and then you married, thus I loathe that you should pass your night alone. And here is your wife." The lady was standing behind him and could not be seen because of his height. He took her by the hand and escorted her past the door and shut it. She fell to the ground out of modesty. I ascertained the door was closed and then placed a bowl of oil and bread in the shadow cast by the lamp, so she could not see how poor a fare I had placed before her.

'I then ascended to the rooftop and called out to the neighbours. I told them the news of my marriage to Sa'īd bin al-Musayyib's daughter and that he had brought her to my house all of a sudden, and that she was there right now. So the people [womenfolk] went to her and the news reached my mother so she also came. She said, "My face is *ḥarām* to your face [i.e. "I will not speak to you"] if you spend the night with her before I have had three days to attend to her and prepare her." So, I waited three days then entered the house with her. She was the most beautiful of all people and the most knowledgeable regarding the book of Allāh, the *Sunnah* of His Messenger ﷺ, and the rights of the husband.' [50]

Such a pious, beautiful, and elegant lady, and her father gives preference to Ạbdullāh bin Abī Wadā'ạ who was a student of knowledge, over al-Walīd who was the heir of the Caliph Ạbd al-Malik and a prince destined to rule, as he was adamant in selecting a person known for his good character and piety. This is giving preference to religiousness and piety, which is a matter slowly fading from our society. This is what the Noble Messenger ﷺ is inclining us towards, to marry and give preference to religious spouses or else be ruined.

Now, the question arises what is piety and religiosity and how can they be recognised in a person? The fact of the matter is that these qualities are often self-evident. When looking for a wife, the outer qualities that point towards religiosity are her *ḥijāb*, *nikāb*, and commitment to praying five times daily. Other, more intrinsic qualities to look for are her *Ịlm* [Islamic knowledge, education, and understanding], and whether she keeps good company, has a good circle of friends, and avoids bad company. Similarly, the qualities to look for in a potential husband are that he is from a pious family, that he prays five times daily, that he is a *ḥāfiz* [one who has memorised

---

[50] Ḥilyah al-Awliyā (Abū Nuạym) Vol. 2: pp.167-168; Tuḥfatul-Ạrūs: pp. 73-74.

the Qur'ān] and/or *Ạālim* [one who has studied the Islamic Sciences], that he is active in the work of *Dạwah* and *Tablīgh*, and that he socialises with and keeps the company of pious and good people. Maybe he has done *bay'ạh* to a *Shaykh* from the *Mashāikh* of *Ḥaqq*.

What is more, thanks to social media, it is very easy to make such background checks on potential spouses and glean information on aspects of their character which would otherwise be difficult to discern. Other, more traditional means of learning about a person is to enquire from their Shaykh if they have made *bay'ạh* to someone, as the Shaykh will be aware of his disciple's spirituality and if they will make a good match for the person. Sometimes, both would-be bride and bridegroom are disciples of the same Shaykh, making it very easy to learn if they are suitable matches for each other, which I have experienced with my own friends. Once you have investigated your potential spouse's character and reputation, if you find them to be pious and religious, then you should arrange for the marriage as soon as possible.

As has been mentioned previously, Abū Hurairah ﵁ and Abū Ḥātim al-Muzanī ﵁ both narrate that the Messenger of Allāh ﷺ said:

إِذَا خَطَبَ إِلَيْكُمْ مَنْ تَرْضَوْنَ دِينَهُ وَخُلُقَهُ فَزَوِّجُوهُ
إِلاَّ تَفْعَلُوا تَكُنْ فِتْنَةٌ فِي الأَرْضِ وَفَسَادٌ عَرِيضٌ .

When there comes to you to propose [to someone under your care] one with whose character and religious commitment you are pleased, then marry [her] to him, for if you do not do so, then there will be turmoil [Fitnah] in the land and widespread corruption and discord [Fasād]. [51]

The word '*khuluq*', which is translated as character here, points towards someone who is generous, humble, has good manners, has a mild and approachable nature, and is one whose friends circle and people who know him and praise him due to his manners and behaviour. In other words, he is not someone who is full of anger, or hatred, or resentment and is not someone who is prone to violence or

[51] Tirmidhī: 1084, 1085; Ibn Mājah: 2043.

is infamous for his ill manners and poor behaviour, and most importantly, he is not stingy and miserly.

WHAT IF PARENTS DON'T AGREE WITH ONE'S CHOICE ?

This is a difficult subject. One needs to step back and view the situation objectively and from both sides. Your parents may have very valid and legitimate reasons or concerns due to some knowledge, information, or experience which they may have regarding that person or family. In such an instance, you should agree with your parents' decision and back down. However, sometimes one or the other may not agree simply because of some personal grudge, for example, the potential spouse is from a related family such as a maternal aunt's son, and your mother is eager for you to marry him but your father refuses because he wants someone from his side of the family. In such a scenario one has to be intelligent and look to work their way around the issue. Talk to your father in a nice and humble way, being respectful of his feelings, using a soft tone, etc. *Inshāllāh*, they will come around through this soft and gentle approach. However, do not disobey your parents or hurt their feelings. Try to keep them happy and follow the Urdu proverb:

سانپ بھی مرے, لاٹھی بھی نہ ٹوٹے-

The snake dies and the club doesn't break.

Be mild and easy with them, and try to get your way without hurting either parent.

MARRYING SOMEONE FROM ANOTHER CASTE

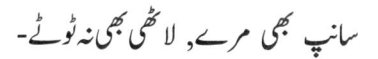

Marrying someone from another caste is not *ḥarām* in Islam, and in itself carries no restrictions. We have many examples in the lives of the *Ṣaḥābah* ﷺ, such as Bilāl bin Rabāḥ al Ḥabashī ﷺ marrying the sister of Ạbdur Rahmān bin Ạwf al Zuhrī ﷺ.[52] Ạbdur Rahmān ﷺ was from the *Banū Zuhrah* from the *Quraysh* tribe and one of the richest of the Companions, whereas Bilāl ﷺ was a freed slave from Abyssinia. Yet when Bilāl ﷺ proposed, as his sister was happy with the match, Ạbdur Rahmān ﷺ gladly approved. There are many other evidences recorded to this effect which all prove that the Noble Prophet ﷺ and his *Ṣaḥābah* ﷺ did not care for the issue of affinity or caste and concentrated instead on a person's faith and piety.[53]

However, looking at our cultural life and customs, sometimes it may be wise to be careful in this regard. For instance, there was an Indian boy who married a Bengali girl. The girl would cook fish and rice every day. The boy pined for *roti* and kebabs and such, but the girl did not know how to cook such foods. This seemingly small matter became an issue of great contention between the two, resulting in many arguments and fights. The matter grew more and more serious until, even though they had two children, they ended up divorcing. One should employ a great amount of foresight and seriously consider whether any such issues could crop up in the future before marrying into a different culture, rather than rush into a marriage because you love her/him. Tragically, we see all too often that love alone is never enough, and so marriage should be made for all the right reasons and with a great deal of foresight and thought. Make life easy for yourself; don't make it hard.

MARRYING A PREVIOUSLY DIVORCED PERSON

The Messenger of Allāh ﷺ married eleven times yet only one wife was a virgin; all the others were either widows or divorcees.

Marrying someone who was married before is encouraged in the *Sharī'ah*. Our present culture has attached such stigma to a divorced woman that no one even considers her, whereas in the true Islamic culture of the *Ṣaḥābah* it was such that as soon as a woman finished

[52] Fatwas of Ibn Bāz Vol.20 pp: 402-403.

[53] Ibid.

her *Iḍda* she would receive multiple proposals. Fāṭima bint Qays was a divorcee, and according to some narrations a widow as well. [54] Yet she was inundated with many proposals and offers of marriage. Amongst them were proposals from the likes of Mu'āwiya bin Abū Sufyān, Abū Jahm bin Hishām and Usāma bin Zaid. When her *Iḍda* period finished, she informed Allāh's Messenger ﷺ and sought his advice regarding the many suitors who had sought for her hand. Allah's Messenger ﷺ said:

أَمَّا أَبُو جَهْمٍ فَلاَ يَضَعُ عَصَاهُ عَنْ عَاتِقِهِ وَأَمَّا مُعَاوِيَةُ فَصُعْلُوكٌ لاَ مَالَ لَهُ انْكِحِي أُسَامَةَ بْنَ زَيْدٍ .

So far as Abū Jahm is concerned, he does not put down his staff from his shoulder [i.e. he is very harsh with women]. So far as Mu'āwiya is concerned, he is a poor man who has no wealth. You should marry Usāma bin Zaid.[55]

Fāṭima bint Qays gestured with her hand, pointing that she did not approve of the idea and objected to him, saying, 'Usāma, Usāma!?' But Allāh's Messenger again told her to marry Usāma bin Zaid and reminded her that obedience to Allāh and obedience to His Messenger was better for her. So she married him and states that:

فَنَكَحْتُهُ فَجَعَلَ اللهُ فِي ذَلِكَ خَيْرًا وَاغْتَبَطْتُ بِهِ وَزَادَ أَبُو بَكْرِ بْنُ أَبِي الْجَهْمِ قَالَتْ فَتَزَوَّجْتُهُ فَشَرَّفَنِي اللهُ بِابْنِ زَيْدٍ وَكَرَّمَنِي اللهُ بِابْنِ زَيْدٍ

So I married him and Allāh put much good and blessings therein, and I was content with him and became an object of envy for others. I married him and Allāh honoured me on account of him and favoured me because of him. [56]

As for men, there is the example of the *Amīr al Mu'minīn*, *Dhun Nūrayn* Uthmān bin Aḍfān ؓ who was first married to the noble daughter of Allāh's Messenger ﷺ Lady Ruqayyah bint Muhammad ؓ [herself a

[54] Muslim: 2942 a.

[55] Muwatta Mālik 29: 1228; Muslim: 1480a, 1480p, 1480q, 1480r; Ibn Mājah 9: 1942.

[56] Muwatta Mālik 29: 1228; Muslim: 1480r.

divorcee]. When she passed away in the second year of *Hijrah* and Ụthmān ﷺ became a widower, Allāh's Messenger ﷺ informed him:

يَا عُثْمَانُ هَذَا جِبْرِيلُ أَخْبَرَنِي أَنَّ اللهَ قَدْ زَوَّجَكَ
أُمَّ كُلْثُومٍ بِمِثْلِ صَدَاقِ رُقَيَّةَ عَلَى مِثْلِ صُحْبَتِهَا .

O Ụthmān, Jibrīl has told me that Allāh has married you to Umm Kulthūm for a dowry like that of Ruqayyah, provided that you treat her as you treated Ruqayyah. [57]

Alas, Lady Umm Kulthūm bint Muḥammad ﷺ also passed away in the ninth year of *Ḥijrah*, upon which Allāh's Messenger ﷺ proclaimed:

لَوْ كَانَتْ عِنْدِي ثَالِثَةٌ زَوَّجْتُهَا عُثْمَانَ وَمَا زَوَّجْتُهُ إِلا بِوَحْيٍ مِنَ السَّمَاءِ .

If I had a third daughter I would have married her to Ụthmān and I have only married him to my daughters through divine revelation. [58]

In other *aḥādīth*, the Noble Prophet ﷺ mentioned that regardless of whether he had ten, forty, or a hundred daughters, he would have given them all in marriage to Ụthmān ﷺ one after the other if each one had died, and that he was pleased with him. [59] The primary qualities that made Ụthmān ﷺ so worthy that he became *Dhun Nūrayn*, 'The Possessor of Two Lights', were his *Ḥayā* – 'the most truly modest of [this *Ummah*] is Ụthmān bin Ạffān ﷺ' [60] - and his generosity. And these are the qualities that we should look for when searching for a partner. Granted, if a man is rich and has his property etc., your daughter may be happy with him, but he should also possess these qualities as well. If he is rich but not religious, you should stay away from him.

---

[57] Ibn Mājah 1: 115.

[58] Tabaqāt al Kubrā (ibn Sạd) Vol. 3; Siyar Ạ'lām al Nubalā 28: 151; Al Mụjamul Kabīr, 11: 490.

[59] Al Mụjamul Awsaṭ: 6112; Al Mụjamul Kabīr 15: 1063; Tārīkh Ibn Ạsākir 39: 43.

[60] Tirmidhī 49: 4159 – 4160; Ibn Mājah 1: 159 -160.

Returning to topic, we can say without doubt that marrying widows or divorcees is encouraged in the *Sharī'ah*. In fact, the great scholar and founder of Dārul Ụlūm Deoband, Maulana Qāsim Nānotwī ﵀, launched a nationwide campaign to emphasise and encourage the remarrying of widows, because in India widows would remain alone for the rest of their lives.

WHAT IF THE PERSON IS RELIGIOUS BUT ISN'T FINANCIALLY STABLE ?

Religiosity and piety are far more important than a strong financial situation. Perhaps a man may not be greatly endowed financially, but if he is religious then everything should be okay. Often it happens that a person gets married and his financial life improves and gets better. This is because all *rizq* and provision is from Allāh ﷻ. When a woman is at her parents' house, it is Allāh ﷻ who provides her *rizq* and provision through her parents; when she moves to her husband's house, Allāh ﷻ will give her *rizq* and provision through her husband, *Inshāllāh*. Moreover, if she is pious, she may even become a reason for the increase of her husband's wealth.

The Messenger of Allāh ﷺ said:

الْتَمِسُوا الرِّزْقَ بِالنِّكَاحِ .

Seek for sustenance in Nikāḥ. [61]

And, according to another narration:

تَزَوَّجُوا النِّسَاءَ فَإِنَّهُنَّ يَأْتِينَكُمْ بِالْمَالِ .

Marry women, for verily they will bring you wealth [through the blessing of Nikāḥ]. [62]

---

[61] Al Maqāṣidul Ḥasanah: 159.

[62] Muṣannaf Ibn Abi Shaybah: 15679.

It is also reported that when a man came to the Prophet ﷺ and complained to him about his state of want and poverty, the Prophet ﷺ told him to marry.[63]

The Prophet ﷺ is also reported to have stated that, "Marriage is the basis for blessings and children are an abundance of mercy." [64]

Allāh ﷻ states in the Qur'ān:

وَاَنْكِحُوا الْاَيَامٰى مِنْكُمْ وَالصّٰلِحِيْنَ مِنْ عِبَادِكُمْ وَاِمَآئِكُمْ ط

اِنْ يَّكُوْنُوْا فُقَرَآءَ يُغْنِهِمُ اللّٰهُ مِنْ فَضْلِهٖ ط وَاللّٰهُ وَاسِعٌ عَلِيْمٌ ۝

Arrange the marriage of the spouseless among you, and the capable from among your bondmen and bondwomen. If they are poor, Allāh will enrich them out of His grace. Allāh is All-Encompassing, All-Knowing. [65]

Ạbdullāh bin Ạbbās ؓ would say regarding this verse, "Allāh Ta'ālā commanded and encouraged them to get married, and he promised them wealth." [66] *Amīr al Mu'minīn* Ụmar bin Al Khattāb ؓ would say:

عَجِبْتُ لِرَجُلٍ لَا يَطْلُبُ الْغِنَى بِالْبَاءَةِ ، وَ اللّٰهُ تَعَالَى يَقُوْلُ فِيْ كِتَابِهِ

إِنْ يَكُونُوا فُقَرَاءَ يُغْنِهِمُ اللّٰهُ مِنْ فَضْلِهِ .

I am surprised at the person who does not search for wealth by means of marriage, whereas Allāh Ta'ālā has stated "If they are poor, Allāh will enrich them out of His grace." [67]

Therefore, we should not crave after those with large amounts of wealth, or spurn the pious and religious due to their current financial instability. If they are in need, then Allāh ﷻ will enrich them through His bounty.

---

[63] Al Maqāṣidul Ḥasanah: 159.

[64] Al Kabāir Li al-Dhahabī.

[65] Qur'ān 24:32.

[66] Tafsīr Ibn Abi Ḥātim; Tafsīr Ibn Kathīr; Al Durrul Manthūr.

[67] Al Maqāṣidul Ḥasanah: 159.

Here we come to the question of having 'their own house', and the importance that is placed on this issue currently. According to the *Sharī'ah*, if the potential husband can provide a private room for the woman, where she can keep her things in privacy and live with ease [change her clothes, relax in comfort without fear of being disturbed, etc.], then that is enough – even if that room is in his parents' house. Then slowly, slowly as they accumulate their money and become financially stronger, they can buy or rent and move into their own house. So, one shouldn't be overly strict in placing this condition or use it as a reason to reject a pious suitor.

There are cases amongst the *Ṣaḥābah* ﷻ, where a Companion did not have much in terms of wealth but the Messenger of Allāh ﷺ told him to marry. Sahl bin Sạd al Sā'ịdi ﷺ narrates that:

جَاءَتِ امْرَأَةٌ إِلَى رَسُولِ الله صلى الله عليه وسلم فَقَالَتْ يَا رَسُولَ الله جِئْتُ أَهَبُ لَكَ نَفْسِي قَالَ فَنَظَرَ إِلَيْهَا رَسُولُ الله صلى الله عليه وسلم فَصَعَّدَ النَّظَرَ فِيهَا وَصَوَّبَهُ ثُمَّ طَأْطَأَ رَسُولُ الله صلى الله عليه وسلم رَأْسَهُ فَلَمَّا رَأَتِ الْمَرْأَةُ أَنَّهُ لَمْ يَقْضِ فِيهَا شَيْئًا جَلَسَتْ فَقَامَ رَجُلٌ مِنْ أَصْحَابِهِ فَقَالَ يَا رَسُولَ الله إِنْ لَمْ يَكُنْ لَكَ بِهَا حَاجَةٌ فَزَوِّجْنِيهَا. فَقَالَ وَهَلْ عِنْدَكَ مِنْ شَيْءٍ . قَالَ لاَ وَالله يَا رَسُولَ الله. فَقَالَ اذْهَبْ إِلَى أَهْلِكَ فَانْظُرْ هَلْ تَجِدُ شَيْئًا . فَذَهَبَ ثُمَّ رَجَعَ فَقَالَ لاَ وَالله مَا وَجَدْتُ شَيْئًا. فَقَالَ رَسُولُ الله صلى الله عليه وسلم انْظُرْ وَلَوْ خَاتَمًا مِنْ حَدِيدٍ . فَذَهَبَ ثُمَّ رَجَعَ فَقَالَ لاَ وَالله يَا رَسُولَ الله وَلاَ خَاتَمًا مِنْ حَدِيدٍ وَلَكِنْ هَذَا إِزَارِي . قَالَ سَهْلٌ مَا لَهُ رِدَاءٌ فَلَهَا نِصْفُهُ . فَقَالَ رَسُولُ الله صلى الله عليه وسلم مَا تَصْنَعُ بِإِزَارِكَ إِنْ لَبِسْتَهُ لَمْ يَكُنْ عَلَيْهَا مِنْهُ شَيْءٌ وَإِنْ لَبِسَتْهُ لَمْ يَكُنْ عَلَيْكَ شَيْءٌ . فَجَلَسَ الرَّجُلُ حَتَّى إِذَا طَالَ مَجْلِسُهُ قَامَ فَرَآهُ رَسُولُ الله صلى الله

عليه وسلم مُوَلِّيًا فَأَمَرَ بِهِ فَدُعِيَ فَلَمَّا جَاءَ قَالَ مَاذَا مَعَكَ مِنَ الْقُرْآنِ .
قَالَ مَعِي سُورَةُ كَذَا وَسُورَةُ كَذَا عَدَّدَهَا. فَقَالَ تَقْرَؤُهُنَّ عَنْ ظَهْرِ قَلْبِكَ
قَالَ نَعَمْ. قَالَ اذْهَبْ فَقَدْ مَلَّكْتُكَهَا بِمَا مَعَكَ مِنَ الْقُرْآنِ.

A woman came to Allāh's Messenger ﷺ and said, "O Allāh's Messenger ﷺ, I have come to present myself to you [in marriage]." Allāh's Messenger ﷺ looked at her. He looked at her carefully, and then lowered his head. When the lady saw that he did not say anything, she sat down. A man from his companions got up and said, "O Allāh's Messenger ﷺ, if you are not in need of her, then marry her to me." The Prophet ﷺ said, "Have you got anything to offer [as mahr]?" The man said, "No, by Allāh, O Allāh's Messenger ﷺ." The Prophet ﷺ said [to him], "Go to your family and see if you have something." The man went and returned, saying, "No, by Allāh, I have not found anything." Allāh's Apostle ﷺ said, "[Go again] and look for something, even if it is a ring from metal." He went again and returned, saying, "No, by Allāh. O Allāh's Messenger ﷺ, I could not find even a metal ring, but this is my Izār [waist sheet]." He had no ridā [upper garment]. He added, "I give half of it to her." Allāh's Messenger ﷺ said, "What will she do with your Izār? If you wear it, she will be naked; if she wears it, you will be naked." So that man sat down for a long while and then got up [to depart]. When Allāh's Messenger ﷺ saw him going, he ordered that he be called back. When he came, the Prophet ﷺ said, "How much of the Qur'ān do you know?" "I know such Sūrah and such Sūrah," he said, counting them. The Prophet ﷺ said, "Do you know them by heart?" He replied, "Yes." The Prophet ﷺ said, "Go, I marry her to you for that much of the Qur'ān which you have." [68]

This indicates that poverty in and of itself is not an impediment to marriage if the husband is religiously committed and trusts sincerely in his Rabb, and the woman is likewise. Based on this hadīth, one opinion of Imām Shāfi'ī ﵀ is that a *Sūrah* of the Qur'ān is sufficient as *mahr*, however Imām Abū Ḥanīfah ﵀ disagrees. After this *hadīth* another is reported which abrogates this *hadīth*, and that is:

---

[68] Bukhārī: 5030, 5087, 5126, 5871; Muslim 1425 a, 1425 b; Tirmidhī: 1114; Abū Dāwūd: 2111; Nasa'ī: 3359.

لا مَهْرَ أَقَلُّ مِنْ عَشْرَةِ دَرَاهِمَ.

There is no mahr less than ten dirhams. [69]

Nevertheless, the above *hadīth* does show that even if a person does not have financial stability, it should not stop them from getting married, as we see in the case of the *Ṣaḥābī* ﷺ who was married and had his wife come live with him. Hence you do not have to be extremely rich in order to marry, and in fact we as a society should lower our demands and preconditions and then, *Inshāllāh,* our society will become clean.

QUALITIES TO LOOK FOR IN A MAN

The following qualities should be sought for and considered when searching for a husband:

[1] *Taqwā* – he should have piety and be religious-minded.

[2] *Ḥalāl income* – he should have a *ḥalāl* income or the ability to earn one in the near future.

[3] Basic Islamic knowledge - he should have at the very least a basic understanding and knowledge of his religion and the rights and responsibilities upon him.

[4] Maturity - he has the mental and emotional maturity and patience to avoid rash actions, and bases decisions on the 'bigger picture', selecting courses of action which will benefit in the long run.

[5] Good family – he is from a respectable family and there is equality between both families' values, stature, and aspirations,

[69] Dāraqutnī: 3603, 3606; Bayhaqī (*Sunan al-Kubrā*): 13935.

which is why oft times marrying a close relation [first or second cousin] is much better.

[6] Generosity – he is kind, good-hearted, and generous with his wealth and affection.

[7] Forgiving nature – he is tolerant, good natured, and forgiving. This and the previous quality can be ascertained from enquiring from his friends and social circles, and the opinions held about him therein.

[8] Purity and cleanliness – he keeps himself clean and tidy and takes care of his appearance.

[9] Responsible nature – he is able to be trusted or depended upon.

[10] Most importantly, he is of the correct *Ạqīdāh*, and is not from any *Bāṭil Firqah* [deviated sects].

QUALITIES TO LOOK FOR IN A WOMAN

The following qualities should be sought for and considered when searching for a wife:

[1] *Taqwā* – she should be pious, god-fearing, and religious-minded.

[2] Affectionate nature – she should be a nice, kind, affectionate and loving person. This loving, affectionate nature is the quality upon which married life survives. Love is like the air in a tyre: if the tyre is punctured, the car will not move forward. If the love is taken out of a marriage, the marriage cannot move forward. It may increase or decrease with the times, but it should never get punctured.

[3] Mildness – she should have an obedient and compliant nature, someone who is non-aggressive and listens to her parents, meaning she will listen to her husband.

[4] Mature-minded – if she is mentally and emotionally mature, she will be able to advise her husband and will not fall prey to rash decisions. As the Arabs say, you should look for one who is virgin in age but mature in wisdom like the oldest woman. A mature and wise wife is a boon from Allāh ﷻ and her advice should be heeded as it will greatly benefit you. Indeed the Mothers of the Believers, the wives of the Prophet Muḥammad ﷺ would often advise him, as was seen with case of Lady Um Salamah رضي الله عنها during the Treaty of Ḥudaybiyyah. Al-Miswar bin Makhrama and Marwān رضي الله عنهما narrate that:

لَمَّا فَرَغَ مِنْ قَضِيَّةِ الْكِتَابِ قَالَ رَسُولُ الله صلى الله عليه وسلم لأَصْحَابِهِ " قُومُوا فَانْحَرُوا، ثُمَّ احْلِقُوا ". قَالَ فَوَاللهِ مَا قَامَ مِنْهُمْ رَجُلٌ حَتَّى قَالَ ذَلِكَ ثَلاَثَ مَرَّاتٍ، فَلَمَّا لَمْ يَقُمْ مِنْهُمْ أَحَدٌ دَخَلَ عَلَى أُمِّ سَلَمَةَ، فَذَكَرَ لَهَا مَا لَقِيَ مِنَ النَّاسِ. فَقَالَتْ أُمُّ سَلَمَةَ يَا نَبِيَّ اللهِ، أَتُحِبُّ ذَلِكَ اخْرُجْ ثُمَّ لاَ تُكَلِّمْ أَحَدًا مِنْهُمْ كَلِمَةً حَتَّى تَنْحَرَ بُدْنَكَ، وَتَدْعُوَ حَالِقَكَ فَيَحْلِقَكَ. فَخَرَجَ فَلَمْ يُكَلِّمْ أَحَدًا مِنْهُمْ، حَتَّى فَعَلَ ذَلِكَ نَحَرَ بُدْنَهُ، وَدَعَا حَالِقَهُ فَحَلَقَهُ. فَلَمَّا رَأَوْا ذَلِكَ، قَامُوا فَنَحَرُوا، وَجَعَلَ بَعْضُهُمْ يَحْلِقُ بَعْضًا، حَتَّى كَادَ بَعْضُهُمْ يَقْتُلُ بَعْضًا غَمًّا.

When the writing of the peace treaty was concluded, Allāh's Messenger ﷺ said to his companions, 'Get up, slaughter your sacrifices, and then shave your heads.' By Allāh, not a man stood from them, even though the Prophet ﷺ repeated his order thrice. When none of them got up, he left them and went to Um Salamah رضي الله عنها and told her of the people's attitude towards him. Um Salamah رضي الله عنها said, "O Prophet of Allāh ﷺ, do you want your order to be carried out? Go out and don't say a word to anyone till you have slaughtered your sacrifice and called your barber to shave your head." So, the Prophet ﷺ went out and did not talk to anyone of them till he did that, i.e. slaughtered the sacrifice and called his barber who shaved his head. Upon seeing this, the noble companions of the Prophet ﷺ got up, slaughtered their sacrifices, and started shaving the heads of one another, and there was so much grief that there was a danger of killing each other due to anguish. [70]

So Um Salamah ﵂ gave a very wise *mashwara* and *Rasūlullāh* ﷺ happily acted accordingly.

Another such incident regarding the wisdom of a mature wife is related by Abū Hurairah ﵁:

قَالَ النَّبِيُّ صلى الله عليه وسلم لأَبِي الْهَيْثَمِ: هَلْ لَكَ خَادِمٌ؟ قَالَ: لاَ، قَالَ: فَإِذَا أَتَانَا سَبْيٌ فَأْتِنَا فَأُتِيَ النَّبِيُّ صلى الله عليه وسلم بِرَأْسَيْنِ لَيْسَ مَعَهُمَا ثَالِثٌ، فَأَتَاهُ أَبُو الْهَيْثَمِ، قَالَ النَّبِيُّ صلى الله عليه وسلم: اخْتَرْ مِنْهُمَا، قَالَ: يَا رَسُولَ اللهِ، اخْتَرْ لِي، فَقَالَ النَّبِيُّ صلى الله عليه وسلم: إِنَّ الْمُسْتَشَارَ مُؤْتَمَنٌ، خُذْ هَذَا، فَإِنِّي رَأَيْتُهُ يُصَلِّي، وَاسْتَوْصِ بِهِ خَيْرًا، فَقَالَتِ امْرَأَتُهُ: مَا أَنْتَ بِبَالِغٍ مَا قَالَ فِيهِ النَّبِيُّ صلى الله عليه وسلم إِلاَّ أَنْ تُعْتِقَهُ، قَالَ: فَهُوَ عَتِيقٌ، فَقَالَ النَّبِيُّ صلى الله عليه وسلم: إِنَّ اللهَ لَمْ يَبْعَثْ نَبِيًّا وَلاَ خَلِيفَةً، إِلاَّ وَلَهُ بِطَانَتَانِ: بِطَانَةٌ تَأْمُرُهُ بِالْمَعْرُوفِ وَتَنْهَاهُ عَنِ الْمُنْكَرِ، وَبِطَانَةٌ لاَ تَأْلُوهُ خَبَالاً، وَمَنْ يُوقَ بِطَانَةَ السُّوءِ فَقَدْ وُقِيَ.

The Prophet ﷺ asked Abū al-Haytham: "Do you have a servant?" "No," he replied. He said, "Come to us when we gain some captives." Incidentally only two captives were brought to the Prophet ﷺ. Abū al-Haytham came to him and the Prophet ﷺ said, "Choose between them." "Choose for me, Messenger of Allah ﷺ," he replied. The Prophet ﷺ said, "The person who is consulted is in a position of trust. Take this one for I have seen him praying. I advise you to treat him well." [Returning home with the servant and having told his wife regarding the Beloved Prophet's ﷺ advice] Abū al-Haytham's wife said [to him], "You will not live up to the words of the Prophet ﷺ concerning him until you set him free." "He is free," he stated. [Upon hearing this] the Prophet ﷺ said, "Allāh did not send a Prophet or Khalīfah except that he has two confidants: a confidant

---

[70] Bukhārī: 2731, 2732.

who commands him to do what is correct and forbids what is bad, and a confidant who will not fall short in corrupting him. Anyone who is protected from the evil confidant has been protected." [71]

Therefore, a wife who can give you advice and help you in matters regarding your religion and responsibilities is someone to be sought for.

[5] Good family – she is from a good family and there is equality between both families' values, stature, and aspirations, which is why oft times marrying a close relation [first or second cousin] is much better.

[6] Purity and cleanliness – she keeps herself clean and tidy and takes care of her appearance.

[7] *Ḥayā* and modesty – she is modest and humble in her bearing.

[8] *Akhlāq*, character and mind-set – she has a kind, well-mannered, and noble personality.

[9] *Housework.* She is fond of housework and would want to keep things neat and clean.

[10] She is sociable and would attend to family at times of family deaths, and other family functions.

THINGS TO AVOID

One should attempt to avoid the transgressor, the bad-tempered, the arrogant, the miser and the stingy, the immature, the one who complains a lot, the criticizer, the excessive talker, and the one who is always reminding you of the favours they have done for you.

[71] Tirmidhī: 2369; Al-Adab Al-Mufrad: 256; Shamā'il Muḥammadīyyah: 52: 372.

Regarding the oft complainer one is reminded of the incident of the prophet Ibrāhīm' s ﷺ advice to his son, the prophet Ismā'īl ﷺ, regarding his wives. Ibn Ạbbās رضي الله عنه narrates:

فَجاءَ إِبْرَاهِيمُ بَعْدَ مَا تَزَوَّجَ إِسْمَاعِيلُ يُطَالِعُ تَرِكَتَهُ ، فَلَمْ يَجِدْ إِسْمَاعِيلَ فَسَأَلَ امْرَأَتَهُ عَنْهُ فَقَالَتْ : خَرَجَ يَبْتَغِي لَنَا – وفي رواية: يصيد لنا – ثُمَّ سَأَلَهَا عَنْ عَيْشِهِمْ وَهَيْئَتِهِمْ فقالت: فَقَالَتْ : نَحْنُ بِشَرٍّ نَحْنُ فِي ضِيقٍ وَشِدَّةٍ ، وَشَكَتْ إِلَيْهِ ، قَالَ: فَإِذَا جَاءَ زَوْجُكِ فَاقْرَئِي عَلَيْهِ السَّلَامَ ، وَقُولِي لَهُ يُغَيِّرْ عَتَبَةَ بَابِهِ ، فَلَمَّا جَاءَ إِسْمَاعِيلُ كَأَنَّهُ آنَسَ شَيْئًا ، فَقَالَ : هَلْ جَاءَكُمْ مِنْ أَحَدٍ ؟ فَقَالَتْ : نَعَمْ . جَاءَنَا شَيْخٌ كَذَا وَكَذَا ، فَسَأَلَنَا عَنْكَ فَأَخْبَرْتُهُ ، وَسَأَلَنِي كَيْفَ عَيْشُنَا فَأَخْبَرْتُهُ أَنَّا فِي جَهْدٍ وَشِدَّةٍ . قَالَ : فَهَلْ أَوْصَاكِ بِشَيْءٍ ؟ قَالَتْ : نَعَمْ . أَمَرَنِي أَنْ أَقْرَأَ عَلَيْكَ السَّلَامَ ، وَيَقُولُ : غَيِّرْ عَتَبَةَ بَابِكَ . قَالَ : ذَاكِ أَبِي ، وَأَمَرَنِي أَنْ أُفَارِقَكِ فَالْحَقِي بِأَهْلِكِ . فَطَلَّقَهَا وَتَزَوَّجَ مِنْهُمْ أُخْرَى ، وَلَبِثَ عَنْهُمْ إِبْرَاهِيمُ مَا شَاءَ اللهُ ، ثُمَّ أَتَاهُمْ بَعْدُ فَلَمْ يَجِدْهُ فَدَخَلَ عَلَى امْرَأَتِهِ فَسَأَلَهَا عَنْهُ فَقَالَتْ : خَرَجَ يَبْتَغِي لَنَا . قَالَ : كَيْفَ أَنْتُمْ ؟ وَسَأَلَهَا عَنْ عَيْشِهِمْ وَهَيْئَتِهِمْ ، فَقَالَتْ : نَحْنُ بِخَيْرٍ وَسَعَةٍ ، وَأَثْنَتْ عَلَى اللهِ، فَقَالَ: مَا طَعَامُكُمْ ؟ قَالَتِ: اللَّحْمُ . قَالَ : فَمَا شَرَابُكُمْ ؟ قَالَتِ : الْمَاءُ . قَالَ : اللَّهُمَّ بَارِكْ لَهُمْ فِي اللَّحْمِ وَالْمَاءِ ، قَالَ النَّبِيُّ صَلَّى اللهُ عَلَيْهِ وَسَلَّمَ: " وَلَمْ يَكُنْ لَهُمْ يَوْمَئِذٍ حَبٌّ ، وَلَوْ كَانَ لَهُمْ حَبٌّ لَدَعَا لَهُمْ فِيهِ فَهُمَا لَا يَخْلُو عَلَيْهِمَا أَحَدٌ بِغَيْرِ مَكَّةَ إِلَّا لَمْ يُوَافِقَاهُ . وفي رواية فَجَاءَ فَقَالَ: أَيْنَ إِسْمَاعِيلُ ؟ فَقَالَتِ امْرَأَتُهُ: ذَهَبَ يَصِيدُ . فَقَالَتْ :

أَلَا تَنْزِلَ فَتَطْعَمَ وَتَشْرَبَ ؟ فَقَالَ : مَا طَعَامُكُمْ وَمَا شَرَابُكُمْ ؟ قَالَتْ : طَعَامُنَا اللَّحْمُ ، وَشَرَابُنَا الْمَاءُ . قَالَ : اللَّهُمَّ بَارِكْ لَهُمْ فِي طَعَامِهِمْ وَشَرَابِهِمْ- قَالَ : فَقَالَ أَبُو الْقَاسِمِ صَلَّى اللهُ عَلَيْهِ وَسَلَّمَ : " بَرَكَةٌ بِدَعْوَةِ إِبْرَاهِيمَ صلى الله عليه وسلم" قَالَ : فَإِذَا جَاءَ زَوْجُكِ فَاقْرَئِي عَلَيْهِ السَّلَامَ ، وَمُرِيهِ يُثَبِّتْ عَتَبَةَ بَابِهِ ، فَلَمَّا جَاءَ إِسْمَاعِيلُ قَالَ : هَلْ أَتَاكُمْ مِنْ أَحَدٍ ؟ قَالَتْ : نَعَمْ . أَتَانَا شَيْخٌ حَسَنُ الْهَيْئَةِ ، وَأَثْنَتْ عَلَيْهِ ، فَسَأَلَنِي عَنْكَ فَأَخْبَرْتُهُ ، فَسَأَلَنِي كَيْفَ عَيْشُنَا فَأَخْبَرْتُهُ أَنَّا بِخَيْرٍ ، قَالَ : فَأَوْصَاكِ بِشَيْءٍ ؟ قَالَتْ : نَعَمْ ، هُوَ يَقْرَأُ عَلَيْكَ السَّلَامَ ، وَيَأْمُرُكَ أَنْ تُثَبِّتَ عَتَبَةَ بَابِكَ . قَالَ : ذَاكِ أَبِي ، وَأَنْتِ الْعَتَبَةُ ، وَأَمَرَنِي أَنْ أُمْسِكَكِ.

"Ibrāhīm ؑ came after Ismā'īl's ؑ marriage in order to see his family that he had left before, but he did not find Ismā'īl ؑ there. When he asked Ismā'īl's ؑ wife about him, she replied: 'He has gone in search of our livelihood.' Then he asked her about their way of living and their condition, and she replied complaining to him: 'We are living in hardship, misery, and destitution.' He said: 'When your husband returns, convey my salutations to him and tell him to change the threshold of the door of his house.' When Ismā'īl ؑ came, he seemed to have perceived something unusual. He asked his wife: 'Did anyone visit you?' She replied: 'Yes, an old man of such and such description came and asked me about you and I informed him, and he asked about our state of living, and, I told him that we were living in hardship and poverty.' Thereupon Ismā'īl ؑ said: 'Did he advise you anything?' She replied: 'Yes, he told me to convey his salutations to you and to change the threshold of your door.' Ismā'īl ؑ said: 'That was my father, and he has ordered me to divorce you. Go back to your family.' So Ismā'īl ؑ divorced her and married another woman from amongst them [i.e. the people of Makkah]. Then Ibrāhīm ؑ stayed away from them for a period as long as Allāh wished, and called on them again but did not find Ismā'īl ؑ. So he came to Ismā'īl's ؑ wife and asked her about him. She said: 'He has gone in search of our livelihood.' Ibrāhīm ؑ asked her about their sustenance and living: 'How are you getting on?' She replied: 'We are prosperous and well off.' Then she praised Allāh, the Exalted. Ibrāhīm ؑ asked: 'What kind of food do you eat?' She said: 'Meat.' He said: 'What do you drink?' She

said: 'Water.' He said, 'O Allāh! Bless their meat and water!'" The Prophet ﷺ added, "At that time they did not have grain, and if they had grain, he would have also invoked Allāh to bless it." The Prophet ﷺ further said, "If somebody has only these two things as his sustenance, his health and disposition will be badly affected because these things do not suit him unless he lives in Makkah." The Prophet ﷺ added, "Then Ibrāhīm 🕮 said to Ismā'īl's 🕮 wife, 'When your husband comes, give my regards to him and tell him that he should keep firm the threshold of his door.' When Ismā'īl 🕮 came back, he asked his wife: 'Did anyone call on you?' She replied: 'Yes, a good looking old man came.' She praised him and added: 'He asked about you, and I informed him, and he asked about our livelihood and I told him that we were in good condition.' Ismā'īl 🕮 asked her: 'Did he give you a piece of advice?' She said: 'Yes, he told me to convey his regards to you and ordered that you should keep firm the threshold of your door.' On that Ismā'īl 🕮 said: 'He was my father and you are the threshold of the door. He has ordered me to keep you with me.'" [72]

In conclusion, one should evaluate his/her priorities regarding a spouse, and if a person is good in terms of religion and character, then one should go ahead with the nikāḥ.

MUHARRAMĀT – THOSE WITH WHOM MARRIAGE IS PROHIBITED

Allāh ﷻ mentions several verses in the Qur'ān:

وَلَا تَنْكِحُوْا مَا نَكَحَ اٰبَآؤُكُمْ مِّنَ النِّسَآءِ اِلَّا مَا قَدْ سَلَفَ ؕ اِنَّهٗ كَانَ فَاحِشَةً وَّمَقْتًا ؕ وَسَآءَ سَبِيْلًا ۝

And marry not those women whom your fathers married, except what hath already happened [of that nature] in the past. Lo! It was ever lewdness and abomination, and an evil way. [73]

[72] Riyāḍ as-Ṣāliḥīn: 19: 1867.

[73] Qur'ān 4:22.

حُرِّمَتْ عَلَيْكُمْ اُمَّهٰتُكُمْ وَبَنٰتُكُمْ وَاَخَوٰتُكُمْ وَعَمّٰتُكُمْ وَخٰلٰتُكُمْ وَبَنٰتُ الْاَخِ
وَبَنٰتُ الْاُخْتِ وَاُمَّهٰتُكُمُ الّٰتِيْٓ اَرْضَعْنَكُمْ وَاَخَوٰتُكُمْ مِّنَ الرَّضَاعَةِ
وَاُمَّهٰتُ نِسَآئِكُمْ وَرَبَآئِبُكُمُ الّٰتِيْ فِيْ حُجُوْرِكُمْ مِّنْ نِّسَآئِكُمُ الّٰتِيْ دَخَلْتُمْ
بِهِنَّ ز فَاِنْ لَّمْ تَكُوْنُوْا دَخَلْتُمْ بِهِنَّ فَلَا جُنَاحَ عَلَيْكُمْ ز وَحَلَآئِلُ اَبْنَآئِكُمُ
الَّذِيْنَ مِنْ اَصْلَابِكُمْ لا وَاَنْ تَجْمَعُوْا بَيْنَ الْاُخْتَيْنِ اِلَّا مَا قَدْ سَلَفَ ط اِنَّ اللّٰهَ
كَانَ غَفُوْرًا رَّحِيْمًا ۝

Forbidden unto you are your mothers, and your daughters, and your sisters, and your father's sisters, and your mother's sisters, and your brother's daughters and your sister's daughters, and your foster-mothers, and your foster-sisters, and your mothers-in-law, and your step-daughters who are under your protection [born] of your women unto whom ye have gone in - but if ye have not gone in unto them, then it is no sin for you [to marry their daughters] - and the wives of your sons who [spring] from your own loins. And [it is forbidden unto you] that ye should have two sisters together, except what hath already happened [of that nature] in the past. Lo! Allāh is ever Forgiving, Merciful. [74]

وَالْمُحْصَنٰتُ مِنَ النِّسَآءِ اِلَّا مَا مَلَكَتْ اَيْمَانُكُمْ ج كِتٰبَ اللّٰهِ عَلَيْكُمْ ج وَاُحِلَّ
لَكُمْ مَّا وَرَآءَ ذٰلِكُمْ اَنْ تَبْتَغُوْا بِاَمْوَالِكُمْ مُّحْصِنِيْنَ غَيْرَ مُسٰفِحِيْنَ ط فَمَا
اسْتَمْتَعْتُمْ بِهٖ مِنْهُنَّ فَاٰتُوْهُنَّ اُجُوْرَهُنَّ فَرِيْضَةً ط وَلَا جُنَاحَ عَلَيْكُمْ فِيْمَا
تَرٰضَيْتُمْ بِهٖ مِنْ م بَعْدِ الْفَرِيْضَةِ ط اِنَّ اللّٰهَ كَانَ عَلِيْمًا حَكِيْمًا ۝

And all married women [are forbidden unto you] save those [captives] whom your right hands possess. It is a decree of Allāh for you. Lawful unto you are all beyond those mentioned, so that ye seek them with your wealth in honest wedlock, not debauchery. And those of whom ye seek content [by marrying them], give unto them their portions as a duty. And there is no sin for you in what ye do by mutual agreement after the duty [hath been done]. Lo! Allāh is ever Knower, Wise. [75]

---

[74] Qur'ān 4:23.

[75] Qur'ān 4:22-24.

There are three forms of relation which render marriage between two people *ḥarām*:

[1] *Nasab* – i.e. lineage, blood-relations, kinship.
[2] *Musāharat* - relation through marriage.
[3] *Radhā'ạt* - milk kinship, formed through suckling/nursing.

Through *Nasab*, seven women become *ḥarām* to marry and vice versa. They are:

[1] Mother.
[2] Daughter.
[3] Sister.
[4] Paternal aunt.
[5] Maternal Aunt.
[6] Niece (brother's daughter).
[7] Niece (sister's daughter).

Through *Musāharat*, the following women become *ḥarām* to marry and vice versa:

[1] Mother-in-law (wife's mother).
[2] Daughter-in-law (son's wife).
[3] Step-daughter (if you have had intimate relations with the mother)
[4] Your wife's sister during your marriage to her (i.e. you cannot marry two sisters together).
[5] To marry women who could be your wife's *maḥrams* were they male (i.e. aunts, nieces, etc.) during your marriage to her. The last two may be married if the wife is divorced.

The reason for the prohibition of marrying to women who are close relations at the same time is due to the fact that it may cause fights between them and create friction and disharmony amongst their family.

As regards to *Radhā'ạt*, all those who are *ḥarām* to marry through *Nasab* are also *ḥarām* through milk kinship. Consequently, you cannot marry your wet-nurse, her daughter, her sister or her husband's sister, or anyone she has breastfed [as they have milk kinship with you].

MARRIAGE TO PEOPLE OF OTHER RELIGIONS

Islamically, people adhering to religions other than Islam can be categorised into two groups: *Ahl al-Kitāb* and non-*Ahl al-Kitāb.*

Ahl al-Kitāb means the people of the earlier scriptures [i.e. the Torah, Psalms, and Bible], literally the People of the Book. These are the Jews and Christians.

As for the non-*Ahl al-Kitāb*, these are the idol-worshippers and fire-worshippers, Hindus, Buddhists, Zoroastrians, etc. who have no actual divine scripture.

From these groups, Islam has a much closer relation to the *Ahl al-Kitāb* and therefore there are certain concessions and flexibility given in regards to them, two of which are mentioned specifically in the Qur'ān. One concession is that their *zabīḥa* [sacrificial meat] may be permissible to eat; the other is that marriage to the women of *Ahl al-Kitāb* may also be permitted. At this point, with regards to the *zabīḥa* or *Nikāḥ* with the *Ahl al-Kitāb*, one must make sure they are actual believing and practicing *Ahl al-Kitāb* who abide by the laws of their divine book, otherwise they will also be out of contention. Whenever Ạbdullāh bin Ụmar was asked regarding this issue, he would advise against marrying Christian women saying:

إِنَّ اللهَ حَرَّمَ الْمُشْرِكَاتِ عَلَى الْمُؤْمِنِينَ، وَلَا أَعْلَمُ مِنَ الْإِشْرَاكِ شَيْئًا
أَكْبَرَ مِنْ أَنْ تَقُولَ الْمَرْأَةُ رَبُّهَا عِيسَى، وَهُوَ عَبْدٌ مِنْ عِبَادِ اللهِ.

Allāh has made it unlawful for the believers to marry Mushrik [polytheist] women, and I do not know of a worse case of Shirk [polytheism] than her saying that 'Īsā is her lord, although he is just one of Allāh's slaves, [76] *while Allāh [has] said:*

وَلَا تَنكِحُوا الْمُشْرِكَاتِ حَتَّىٰ يُؤْمِنَّ ۚ

Do not marry the polytheist women, unless they come to believe [in Islam]." [77] [78]

Ụmar bin al-Khaṭṭāb ﷺ also did not approve of such marriages and would oppose them without going to the length of stating they were forbidden. It is well known that he ordered a number of Ṣaḥābah, including Ṭalḥā bin Ụbaidullāh ﷺ and Ḥudhaifah bin al-Yamān ﷺ, who had married *Ahl al-Kitāb* women to divorce their non-Muslim wives, fearing that such practice would be followed by other Muslims and leading to them choosing women from the people of the book to the extent of abandoning marrying Muslim women, or for similar reasons. [79]

After the passing of Salmān al-Fārsī ﷺ, Ḥudhaifah bin al-Yamān ﷺ was appointed as governor of Madāin. When Ḥudhaifah ﷺ came to Madāin, he married a Jewish woman. Ụmar ﷺ learned of this and wrote a letter to him asking him to divorce the woman. Ḥudhaifah bin al-Yamān ﷺ wrote back asking, "Is she unlawful for me? If you consider her *ḥarām* [unlawful] for me, then I will leave her." In reply, Ụmar ﷺ wrote, "I am not saying that she is unlawful, but women from these people do not have chastity, therefore I apprehend lest immodesty and humiliation [and morals contrary to those in Islam] enter into your household [through her]." [80] In another narration, Ụmar ﷺ replied, "She is a live coal and I ordered you to divorce her." Ḥudhaifah ﷺ again wrote back, "Do you consider her *ḥarām* [unlawful] for me?" Ụmar ﷺ replied, "She is a live coal." Ḥudhaifah

---

[76] Bukhārī: 5285.

[77] Qur'ān 2: 221.

[78] Tafsīr Ibn Kathīr.

[79] Tafsīr ibn Kathīr, verse 2:221.

[80] Jāmị al-Bayān, 2: 376-378; Aḥkām al-Qur'ān, 1: 333.

said, "I know she is a live coal; and she is lawful for me to get married to." [81]

When Umar wrote another letter to Hudhaifah his words were: "I hereby put you on oath that you will – before you put down this letter from your hands – divorce and release her, as I fear other Muslims will begin following your example and begin choosing women from among the People of the Book because of their beauty [bypassing Muslim women in the process]. What greater trial could there be for Muslim women?" [82]

On the one hand, there is the legality and permissibility of marrying a woman of the *Ahl al-Kitāb*, as long as she is a practicing and believing *Ahl al-Kitāb*, however, on the other hand there is the moral duty you have to your children and grandchildren to protect their *Īmān*, as well as your own. Who is to say whether this marriage remains stable and your feelings stay mutual? What happens if you are separated or divorced and she takes custody of the children? What effect will having a non-Muslim parent and grandparents have on your children? Many times it has been seen that even the women who embrace Islam and live for many years as Muslims turn back and fall into their old habits and old ways. I even know of a case where the woman embraced Islam and lived with her husband for thirty years, before turning her back on him and her faith and eloping with her old high school boyfriend. Even old age and decades spent with him as a Muslim did not stop her from betraying her husband.

To conclude this topic, we will not declare *ḥarām* what Allāh has made *ḥalāl*. However, there are certain conditions and considerations which need to be very carefully addressed when making this leap. It should be ensured she is an actual, believing, and practicing Christian or Jew, rather than someone who only 'identifies' as Christian or Jewish because of her heritage or community and is actually an agnostic materialist. After this, one should seriously think through the moral implications of such a step, as such a marital relation may

---

[81] Al-Mughnī.

[82] Kitāb al-Āthār: 156; Mā'riful Qur'ān: 80-81.

cause the religious and moral corruption of both the man and his future progeny.

ARRANGED MARRIAGES

Often, when people talk of arranged marriages, they misperceive two separate actions and confuse them as one: arranging a marriage and forcing a marriage.

Forced marriages, the horror stories we hear of people being forced to travel to another country and coerced into marrying someone from their parents' village, are not allowed, impermissible and forbidden. Such marriages are often harmful to all parties involved and parents should never take such action. Most times the two people are not compatible with one another, with their manners, upbringing, education, attitudes, and ideas being completely different. Such marriages rarely survive. Do not force anyone against their will.

An arranged marriage is when parents look for suitable marriage partners for their children and present the choice before them, taking into consideration their son's or daughter's personality and what will be beneficial for their future.

Shaykh Yūnus Jaunpūrī ﷺ states that there are two types of *Nikāḥ*: *Ịshq* [love] marriages and those arranged by parents. From these two, the Shaykh posits that the love marriage rarely survives, because *Ịshq* is based on *fisq* [breaking Allāh's command]. When you enter into a relationship before marriage, you are already in *fisq*, kissing, hugging, maybe even fornicating, it can never survive because the basis and foundation is so weak. Alternatively, in arranged marriages as the parents carefully look for a suitable partner, this marriage generally survives. There may be exceptions, but this is usually the case. Shaykh Yūnus ﷺ gives the reason for this asserting that because the parents have arranged the marriage and tried their best to find a suitable match, if the marriage ever hits dire straits their heartfelt *duās* help the marriage survive.

In the US, a Libyan brother named Ibrāhīm who often lectured on Islam in churches, schools, and colleges was asked a question regarding the prevalence of arranged marriages in the Muslim community. A young lady stood up and asked, 'What kind of people are you? You make your girls marry complete strangers and say they have to go and start living together, even though they're total strangers and don't know each other.'

Ibrāhīm responded with a question of his own asking, 'Of all the girls and women seated here, how many of you have been in a relationship at least three, four, or five times and then have had those relationships break down?' Many of the women raised their hands in response. 'So,' he said, 'Do you see? That is the problem. You have a habit of falling into love, into a relationship, hoping he's finally "the one", and then after sometime it all falls apart. You break up. And then you begin another relationship, and when it doesn't work, another relationship. And the cycle continues. You develop this habit of breaking up and so no relationship can survive.'

'Whereas with us, we look for a suitable partner for our children based on their personalities and characteristics who we hope will match well with them. If they say no, we don't force them but rather help them find another suitable match towards whom they are more inclined. And once they are married, they have the mentality that they have to stay with their partner and work together to make it work for the rest of their lives. So they stick together through thick and thin, but you have developed this habit of making and breaking, making and breaking. 'Whereas our youngsters don't know how to make and break relationships so they stick together. This is why divorce rates are very high among you but low among us.' [83]

Consequently, if you find someone you like, involve your parents as early as possible to ensure there is clarity and so both parents can make sure the match is suitable and arrange the marriage as quickly as possible.

FINDING THE RIGHT SPOUSE

THROUGH THE CORRECT CHANNELS

One should avoid chat-lines, online forums, and dating sites as the water there is much muddied and it is difficult to judge the depths.

---

[83] Ibrāhīm.

Similarly, while marriage forums, matrimonial agencies, and marriage events can be helpful and lead to a good match, it is best to stick to the traditional routes and methods of finding a spouse.

IMPORTANCE OF MAKING LOTS OF DUĀ BEFORE MARRIAGE

When looking for a spouse, one should make lots of duā. Pray lots of *Ṣalātul Ḥājat* and *Ṣalātul Istikhāra*. There are some *wazāif* that are beneficial for this as well.

One *wazīfa* that I have often given to people looking to get married is, for girls once they are pure from menstruation and for boys anytime, for forty continuous nights to sit down after *Eshā ṣalāh* and before they sleep, repeat the following names of Allāh ﷻ 1111 [one thousand, one hundred and eleven] times:

يَا لَطِيْفُ يَا وَدُوْدُ۔

Inshāllāh, Allāh ﷻ will provide a suitable partner.

Hadhrat Shaykh [Muḥammad Zakariyyā ؒ] was asked for a *wazīfa* for this purpose and he recommended that the mother and daughter sit facing the *Qiblah* and repeat the *Durūd Ibrāhīmī* 500 times in a single sitting. Also, the following Qur'ānic duās should be repeated daily as well:

رَبَّنَآ اٰتِنَا فِى الدُّنْيَا حَسَنَةً وَّفِى الْاٰخِرَةِ حَسَنَةً وَّقِنَا عَذَابَ النَّارِ ۝ [84]

And

رَبَّنَا هَبْ لَنَا مِنْ اَزْوَاجِنَا وَذُرِّيّٰتِنَا قُرَّةَ اَعْيُنٍ وَّاجْعَلْنَا لِلْمُتَّقِيْنَ اِمَامًا ۝ [85]

And

رَبِّ اِنِّىْ لِمَآ اَنْزَلْتَ اِلَيَّ مِنْ خَيْرٍ فَقِيْرٌ ۝ [86]

---

[84] Qur'ān 2:201.

[85] Qur'ān 25:74.

[86] Qur'ān 28:24.

SALĀTUL ISTIKHĀRA

Istikhāra means to seek goodness and benefit from Allāh ﷻ within an action or decision. *Ṣalātul Istikhāra* can be prayed before meeting a potential spouse as well as after and at any time of the day or night, provided it is not during the three prohibited times [after *Fajr*, after *Asr*, and *Zawāl* time]. One should preferably pray it for several days before meeting the potential spouse. An important thing to remember concerning *Ṣalātul Istikhāra* is to keep an open mind. If you have already made your mind up, then there is no point in doing *Istikhāra.*

Having prayed *Ṣalātul Istikhāra* beforehand, there is another smaller *duā* of *Istikhāra* that one can pray during the meeting with your potential spouse. The Mother of the Believers, Lady Ā'ishah ؓ narrated from Abū Bakr As-Siddīq ؓ that whenever the Prophet ﷺ intended to take an action, he would say:

اللّٰهُمَّ خِرْ لِي وَاخْتَرْ لِي.

O Allāh, make it good for me and choose for me. [87]

This *duā* should be repeated eleven times during the meeting. Moreover, one should make a habit of using this *duā* whenever making any decision.

Overall, when meeting a spouse, one should try to be prepared and be confident and make their enquiries beforehand. Just as when you are going to a meeting or a job interview, you check your responsibilities and the requirements and prepare for potential questions beforehand, so you should also do this when meeting a potential spouse. The meeting and *Istikhāra* are just a support to the main concern which is making sure they are suitable and compatible for spending the rest of your life with.

[87] Tirmidhī: 3516.

WHAT QUESTIONS TO ASK A POTENTIAL SPOUSE ?

Firstly, it should be clarified that in this case less is always better. Do not put off a potential partner by plaguing them with too many questions. The less you talk the better. I know of a case where a Sri-Lankan brother refused a proposal because he was extremely put off after meeting a girl due to her having prepared a massive list of detailed questions and putting him through an excruciatingly long interview. Do not go in with an interview sheet of questions. You should already have done your 'homework' on the person and the meeting is there so you can see each other, rather than to get an exhaustive account of the person's past, present, and future.

Moreover, meeting each other is not *Fardh* or *wājib*; it is not necessary. It is permissible, or we can say at most *Mustaḥab*. Bakr bin Ạbdullāh Al-Muzanī ﵁ narrates that:

عَنِ الْمُغِيرَةِ بْنِ شُعْبَةَ أَنَّهُ خَطَبَ امْرَأَةً فَقَالَ النَّبِيُّ ﷺ "انْظُرْ إِلَيْهَا فَإِنَّهُ أَحْرَى أَنْ يُؤْدَمَ بَيْنَكُمَا" .

Al-Mughīra bin Shụ'bah ﵁ proposed to a woman, so the Prophet ﷺ said [to him] "Look at her, for indeed that is more likely to make love and affection last between the two of you." [88]

So he did that and married her, and mentioned how well he got along with her. [89] Jābir bin Ạbdullāh ﵁ narrates:

قَالَ رَسُولُ اللهِ ﷺ " إِذَا خَطَبَ أَحَدُكُمُ الْمَرْأَةَ فَإِنِ اسْتَطَاعَ أَنْ يَنْظُرَ إِلَى مَا يَدْعُوهُ إِلَى نِكَاحِهَا فَلْيَفْعَلْ " قَالَ فَخَطَبْتُ جَارِيَةً فَكُنْتُ أَتَخَبَّأُ لَهَا حَتَّى رَأَيْتُ مِنْهَا مَا دَعَانِي إِلَى نِكَاحِهَا وَتَزَوُّجِهَا فَتَزَوَّجْتُهَا .

---

[88] Tirmidhī: 1087.

[89] Ibn Mājah: 1938.

The Prophet ﷺ said, "When one of you asked a woman in marriage, if he is able to look at what will induce him to marry her, he should do so." Jābir ؓ adds, "So I asked a girl in marriage, and I would hide at some place to have a glance at her, until what I saw of her induced me to marry her, and so I married her." [90]

Mullāh Ạlī Qārī (d. 1014 AH/1605 CE) quotes Ạllāmah Ṭībī's (d. 743 AH/1342 CE) assertion that the meaning of "that which will induce him to marry her" is her wealth, status, beauty, and religion [*Dīn*]." [91] Another *hadīth* is narrated by Abū Hurairah ؓ regarding a man intended to marry a woman and consulted the Prophet ﷺ, who advised:

أُنْظُرْ إِلَيْهَا فَإِنَّ فِي أَعْيُنِ الأَنْصَارِ شَيْئًا وَ فِيْ رِوَايَةٍ

أَلاَ نَظَرْتَ إِلَيْهَا فَإِنَّ فِي أَعْيُنِ الأَنْصَارِ شَيْئًا ۔

Look at her, for there is something in the eyes of the Anṣār.[92]

Mullāh Ạlī Qārī (d. 1014 AH/1605 CE) also states that if it is not viable for you to see her or you want to avoid it then a female member of your family, such as your mother or sister, can be sent to view her on your behalf. [93] This makes it clear that actually physically seeing each other is neither *Fardh* nor *wājib*, and what should be focused on is finding enough information that would suggest you are compatible with each other. Furthermore, if you are living in different countries and want to see one another before the marriage, then you can use FaceTime, Skype, or Google Hangouts to video call for this purpose.

Once you have seen each other and agreed to marry, you cannot keep seeing each other and should instead wait till the *Nikāḥ*. Seeing each other once before marriage should be enough.

---

[90] Abū Dāwūd: 2082; Musnad Aḥmad: 14176; Mustadrak-ạlā-Ṣaḥīḥayn: 1117.

[91] Mirqāt al-Mafātīḥ: 6/256.

[92] Nasa'ī: 3246, 3247.

[93] Mirqāt al-Mafātīḥ: 6/251.

REVEALING ONES PREVIOUS MARITAL STATUS

This is necessary and must be done. A number of *aḥādīth* state to the effect that:

مَنْ غَشَّنَا فَلَيْسَ مِنَّا .

He who has acted dishonestly towards us [deceived us] is not of us. [94]

Therefore, if you portray yourself as unmarried when in fact you have been previously married [or are still married], you are lying and deceiving the other person. If you have been married before then you should mention it and make the other person aware. Everything should be clear between the two people who intend to marry.

DISCLOSING ONE'S SINS TO ONE ANOTHER

This is not necessary unless it is something major which would affect the marriage. We all make mistakes. If it is something in your past that you have repented from and left behind, then there is no need to bring it up. One needs to be intelligent in this matter and apply his/her wisdom to the situation. There is no need to bring up every little detail of your entire history. As long as you don't deceive or mislead the person you should be okay. You do not need to tell them everything.

HOW TO MAKE YOUR DECISION ?

Once you have made *Istikhāra* and *Istishāra* [consulted the opinions of family, Shaykh, etc.] and have been told that it is a good match, then you should move forward with it and be positive.

---

[94] Muslim: 101, 102; Tirmidhī: 1315, 4307; Abū Dāwūd: 3452; Ibn Mājah: 2309.

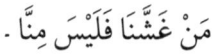

DISCUSSING LIVING ARRANGEMENTS

There is no harm in asking about living arrangements and whether you will be staying with parents or in a separate property. However, it is advisable to not make this a priority, i.e. that you will only marry them if they live separately. If you have to live with the parents, you should live with the parents and take his parents as your own parents. You will get the *thawāb* [reward] for their *khidmat* [attending and serving them] as you would for the *khidmat* of your own parents. In fact, in today's climate, I would say that living with parents is better as it is much easier in caring for children and easing burdens. So, if you can, then this is more advisable as there is more opportunity to earn *thawāb* and also to free up some burdens. What is more, it will also please and keep the husband happy as well. Later, once you have more children and if the property is small, then you can buy or rent your own property. The key is to be understanding and not put pressure on the matter of staying separately or living together. This is not a be-all and end-all matter.

THE DEFINITION OF ENGAGEMENT

Engagement is an oral promise, i.e. giving your word that you are happy and will marry in the near future. The other aspects that surround this, such as handing out sweetmeats, giving an engagement ring, giving of clothes and presents, making it into a specific event, these are all permissible but not necessary. Rather, over indulging in these traditions and customs and spending a lot of time and money on making preparations for the engagement is a bad practice and is an act of thriftless wastefulness, extravagance, and squandering. So one can display their happiness on such an occasion and celebrate it to a certain extent, but staying within the limits of the *Sharī'ah* is always best.

THE ENGAGEMENT RING

The environment has become such that girls often require or demand an engagement ring. However, there is the danger of *tashabbuh* [resemblance] of the practices of other religions. They say that the engagement ring should be worn on the third finger, and then the wedding ring replaces it. This is a Christian practice of representing the trinity. In fact, we have convoluted our Islamic practices with various eastern and western cultural customs borrowed from other faiths. Many Hindu and Christian traditions have been adopted by people unknowingly, and one should learn about these customs and try to avoid engaging in them. A good place to start is Ismail Adam Patel's book, *An Invitation towards Understanding Wedding Customs*.

Therefore, whilst engagement rings are permissible do not make them necessary. Instead of an engagement ring, you could give some money so she can buy whatever she wants with that. It is always good to give gifts before the marriage and the Noble Qur'ān defines this as *matā'*:

مَتَاعٌ م بِالْمَعْرُوْفِ ط حَقًّا عَلَى الْمُتَّقِيْنَ ○

An honourable a provision in kindness: being an obligation on the God-fearing.[95]

THE PERIOD OF BEING ENGAGED

The less time spent being engaged before marriage the better. Do not over extend this period and make it too long. Engagement now and wedding after one year and *rukhsatī* after two years . . . what is the point of this delay? These things should happen in quick succession: engagement, *Nikāḥ*, *rukhsatī*. Done.

BREAKING OFF AN ENGAGEMENT

This happens if the wedding is delayed, so one should not delay the wedding. However, if you do need to break it off for some reason, such as you discover some bad habits or illness that changes perceptions, then do so gracefully and with the utmost respect. There is nothing wrong with this *per se*, if you decide upon this course of action. Hadhrat Abū Bakr ﷺ broke off the engagement of Lady Ā'ishah ﷺ to

[95] Qur'ān 2:241.

Jubair bin Mut'ịm ﷺ before her marriage to the Messenger of Allāh ﷺ. Therefore this can be done.

RETURNING GIFTS IF THE ENGAGEMENT IS BROKEN OFF

If the gift is something expensive and they ask for it to be returned, then you should do so. This is a ruling concerning *hadya* and *hibā*, wherein if you give a gift to someone then it is not right to ask for it to be returned. It is *makrūh* [disliked] but not *ḥarām*. For example, if you gifted an expensive pen to someone but later regret the decision, you can ask them to return it but ultimately the choice is theirs to do whatever they will. So, it is *makrūh* to ask for the return of a gift, but if someone does ask for it, then it is better to return it.

Now if many expensive gifts were given during the engagement – a golden ring, platinum ring, etc. – and they ask for them to be returned as they need to find another partner for their son and marry him elsewhere, then you should give it back. Similarly, if the girl's side had given some expensive gifts e.g. watch or pen etc., they could also ask for you to return these gifts back to them.

GIVING JEWELLERY AND CLOTHES AS GIFTS TO EACH OTHER'S FAMILIES

This is going beyond the limits. It is one thing to gift the bride-to-be or groom-to-be, but buying clothes and gifts for all their family members is an act of wasteful extravagance and squandering. Moreover, many times people cannot afford it and have to go out of their way to buy expensive gifts for each other's families. Whilst it is permissible, one should stay within the limits and within their own means, only doing as much as can be easily done and not go beyond that.

ISLAMIC PRACTICES VS CULTURAL PRACTICES

Wedding cakes, sherbet drinks, mehndi, stag party, hen party, etc. So many practices from other cultures have diluted our Islamic practices and made things complicated. Islam does not teach us any of these things. Islamically, have an engagement quickly followed by *Nikāḥ* and *rukhsatī* and done. They can start living together and building their lives.

FALLING IN LOVE

If someone falls in love with another person, the number one advice to them is to first and foremost control their emotions. Do not let your emotions surpass beyond the limits of reason by constantly thinking or daydreaming about them, listening to love songs, chatting to them, or 'following' them via social media. If your emotions do get out of control, and your thoughts are overcome by your love for the person, talk to your parents and if they agree, get married and live with each other. This is what is meant in the following *hadīth:*

لَمْ نَرَ لِلْمُتَحَابَّيْنِ مِثْلَ النِّكَاحِ .

There is nothing like marriage, for two people who love one another. [96]

This *hadith* shows that *Nikāḥ* increases the love between two people, so if two people love each other and they get married, their love will increase. And through marriage we should try to increase their love and let them live in harmony and peace. This is a beautiful *hadīth* of the Messenger of Allāh ﷺ showing that he knows well the hearts of youngsters and advising parents that if this scenario happens and they are compatible, you should marry them.

Compatibility is important and means of similar age, family, and religiosity. If they are not compatible, then parents should explain to them why, and get them to relent. This scenario actually occurred where a girl of sixteen eloped with a man of twenty eight who was a

[96] Ibn Mājah: 1920.

known drug addict. Her parents sought to help her and talked with the man's family but they would not agree to separate them. Eventually, the matter went to the courts, and even the judge tried to dissuade her from her course of action but she would not relent. Eventually, the man showed his true colours and began to beat her. She contacted her uncle who took her from there and reunited her with her parents. Where there is unsuitability, you should stop, as this love is no good and will lead to misery. However, where there is suitability, their parents should get them married as this will increase their love and happiness and save them from sin.

There is a story of the second Abbasid caliph, Abū Jạ'far Ạbdullāh ibn Muḥammad al-Manṣūr - (d. 158 AH/775 CE), who on the way to the *Ḥajj* pilgrimage set up camp for the night in one place when a young man approached him and asked for his help. The young man informed him that he was in love with his cousin and she was very much in love with him. However, her father intended to marry her off to someone rich and wealthy. He requested the caliph to speak on his behalf. Abū Jạ'far al-Manṣūr ﷺ straightaway summoned the boy's father and uncle and explained the situation to them, telling them to not become a barrier between their children's love. They submitted to the caliph's command and he immediately performed the *Nikāḥ*, gave ten thousand dirhams as a dowry gift for the bride, and made arrangements for a *Walīma* to take place the next morning. This is what the Beloved Prophet ﷺ said:

مِنْ أَفْضَلِ الشَّفَاعَةِ أَنْ يُشَفَّعَ بَيْنَ الِاثْنَيْنِ فِي النِّكَاحِ .

One of the best kinds of intercession is interceding between two people concerning marriage. [97]

When you see that a boy and a girl like each other, but their parents or some other family members are being an obstruction to it, one should approach the *Imām* or leader of the community to intervene and talk to both parties and get them married. This is the best kind of

[97] Ibn Mājah: 2051.

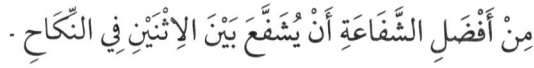

intercession and what is missing from our society today. In the olden days, we had elders in the community who would do this work for free. They would help families in searching for suitable partners.

Moreover, one should be very careful in the matter of love and keep one's self in control, for no one knows when or through what cause or action it may develop. It does not take long to fall in love and people can fall in love very easily. There is a legend told of the Mughal emperor Jahāngīr (d. 1036 AH/1627 CE) and how he first met and fell in love with his future wife, the empress Nūr Jahān (d. 1054 AH/1645 CE). Jahāngīr, at the time merely Prince Salīm, was walking, so the story goes, through a garden. He had just returned from Mina Bazaar and was carrying two doves. He came across some beautiful flowers which he wished to pick but needed someone to hold his doves in order to do so. It was then he first saw Mehr-an-Nisā [Nūr Jahān's original name], the daughter of his father's Persian minister, sitting forlorn on the edge of a garden fountain. Prince Salīm asked her to hold his doves while he went to pick flowers. Yet, returning presently, flowers in hand, he found one of the doves gone and only a single bird in her hands. 'What happened to the other dove?' Prince Salīm asked. 'It flew off,' she said. 'How did that happen?' the prince demanded. 'Like this,' she replied, releasing the second dove into the air from where it also fluttered off. Rather than becoming angry at the loss of his doves, Prince Salīm became captivated by the young lady's wit and charm. [98]

Shaykh Nizāmuddīn Auliyā (d. 725AH/1325CE) would often say, 'The laundress's son was more fortunate than us. I couldn't even do that much.' His disciples asked him as to who this laundress's son was and how he mattered. So he told them that there was once a laundress who would receive bundles of clothes from the royal palace to be laundered. The laundress and her husband would wash and iron the clothes and then take them back to the palace. They also had a son,

[98] Christensen, T. (2012) *1616: The World in Motion*, Counterpoint Press: Berkeley California.
Findly, E.B. (1993) *Nūr Jahan, Empress of Mughal India*, Oxford U.P.: Oxford
Villiers Stuart, C.M. (2006) *Gardens of the Great Mughals*, (online) Gardenvisit.com.

who as he grew up, began to join his parents in their daily washing chores at the river bank. The clothes that were received from the palace contained a few garments belonging to the princess. Attractive and pricey as they were, the young man would think of the princess who wore them. He would separate them from the lot, take them into his custody, lavish all his attention on them, and press and fold them carefully to be carried to the palace. And through these clothes the boy fell in love with the princess, though he had never set eyes on her. Given that he occupied a far lower rung of the social ladder, there was not even a remote chance for an encounter with his love.

This continued for some time until his mother began to notice what he was doing. She confided in her husband her worry that their son's love for the princess would bring ruin to the whole family. So the father forbade the son from doing anymore laundry. While the son had been doing some service for his beloved, it had worked to let off steam and keep the fever of his passion for the princess under control. But when he was forbidden from this service, his love found no outlet and no way to express itself. So he fell severely ill and died.

When the quality of the washing and the style of folding of the princess's clothes changed, she sent for the laundress and asked her who was responsible for her clothes. The laundress replied, 'Your Highness, it is I.' 'Who would wash them before you?' the princess asked. 'It was I all along,' said the laundress. 'Fold these clothes.' commanded the princess. But the laundress could not fold as her son used to. 'You are lying. Who used to wash my clothes before? Tell me the truth or I'll have you punished!' ordered the princess. The laundress saw no way out except by telling the truth and her heart was also overflowing with grief at the death of her son. So she began to cry and told the princess everything. The princess was stunned. She asked for the royal carriage to be brought and filled a basket with flowers. Then she went to the grave of the boy who had sacrificed his life in his love for her and laid the flowers at his grave. During the rest of her life she continued to visit the boy's grave every year on the anniversary of his death and lay flowers at his grave.

After relating this story, Shaykh Nizāmuddīn Auliyā said, 'If it is possible to fall in love with a human being whom one has never seen then why isn't it possible to love Allāh ﷻ without seeing Him? If the love of a human being can change one's temperament and one can pour all one's abilities and love into washing their clothes and folding them nicely, then why can't we pour our love for Allāh ﷻ into our worship of Him and worshipping nicely? But instead of our prayers having our heart and soul in them they weigh on us like burdens. If a princess can recognize clothes that have been folded with love, will Allāh ﷻ not be able to differentiate between prayers that have our love for Him in them and prayers that we throw off as yokes? The laundress's son was successful because his love found acceptance while we do not know whether our worship will be accepted or thrown back at us. In the same way that Allāh ﷻ demands faith, prayers and fasts, He demands our love too. This love is not recommended but required of us. Yet we are ignorant of it. I swear by Allāh ﷻ, that if these prayers had not been commissioned then the hearts of those who love Allāh ﷻ would burst in the same way that the heart of the laundress's son burst from not being able to express his love. The night-long prayers are not possible without the emotion behind them that keeps one standing. Allāh ﷻ prescribed prayers upon seeing the condition of His Messenger's ﷺ heart and asked him to pray throughout the night and keep repeating His words to find comfort. That is why when prayer time would commence, the Messenger of Allāh ﷺ would ask Bilāl رضي الله عنه to call the Adhān saying, "Give us comfort by it, O Bilāl."'

To conclude this subject of falling in love, we can sum up by saying first and foremost be careful, be cautious, for love can form from the most random of acts or loosest of associations. If you do fall in love, and the person is of an acceptable and compatible background and personality then do get married. Talk to both of your families and try to work something out, and don't be too hard or harsh towards your parents as they only want what is best for you. *Inshāllāh* some path will be paved out for you.

MUT'AH

Nikāḥ Mut'ạh is a temporary marriage, where you marry someone for a fixed period be it a number of years, months, or even days. Sometimes students studying abroad marry someone for the duration of their study. This is not allowed. It is *ḥarām* and a major sin. All four schools of the *Ahlus Sunnah wal Jamā'ạh* are unanimous on this. *Nikāḥ* is for life; not temporary, but permanent. The intention should be to stay with one another for the rest of your lives. In fact, the only community which believe it to be permissible are the *Ithnā'ạshariyyah* [Twelver] sect of the Shia who deem it to carry great reward.

It is the *Ithnā'ạshariyyah* sect's preposterous belief that one who engages in *Mut'ạh* once in his lifetime reaches the status of Imām Al-Ḥussain. One who engages in it twice becomes equal in status to Imām Al-Ḥasan. The one who performs it three times reaches the position of Imām Ạlī. And he who practices it four times acquires the level and position of the Prophet Muhammad ﷺ.[99] This fabricated narration is in their books, whereas it is the doctrine of the *Ahlus Sunnah* that no one can reach the ranks of Imām Al-Ḥasan ﵁ and Imām Al-Ḥussain ﵁, as they are from amongst the *Ṣaḥābah* and the *Ahl Al-Bayt*.

In Iran the Shia clerics promote this practice, which has had adverse effects on their society. Dr Donna M. Hughes, citing an official source in Tehran, states:

> '... There has been a 635% increase in the number of teenage girls in prostitution, or rather, *Mut'ạh*. The magnitude of this statistic conveys how rapidly this form of abuse has grown. In Tehran, there are an estimated 84,000 women and girls in prostitution, many of them are on the streets, others are in the 250 brothels that reportedly operate in the city. The trade is also international: thousands of Iranian women and girls have been "contracted in *Mut'ạh*" to foreigners abroad. The head of Iran's Interpol

[99] Furū' al-Kāfī.

> bureau believes that the *Mut'ạh* trade is one of the most profitable activities in Iran today.
>
> 'High unemployment – 28% for youth 15-29 years of age and 43% for women 15-20 years of age – is a serious factor in driving restless youth to accept *Mut'ạh*. The *Mut'ạh* "pimps" take advantage of any opportunity in which women and children are vulnerable. For example, following the recent earthquake in Bam, orphaned girls have been contracted out in Tehran where Iranian and foreign traders meet.' [100]

Mut'ạh is *ḥarām* but unfortunately on our university campuses many Sunni Muslim girls are lured into engaging in it by Shia boys. There are accounts of a certain university campus where Muslim girls are engaging in *Mut'ạh* for one night. May Allāh ﷻ protect our daughters and our youth!

NIKĀḤ MISYĀR

Nikāḥ Misyār, from the route word '*seyr*' ['to travel' or 'go along'], is a specific type of matrimonial arrangement wherein all the requirements are met for a *Nikāḥ*, with the addition that the spouses give up some of their rights by mutual consent, such as the wife's right to housing and financial support, etc. The *Nikāḥ* is done but they both live with their parents and from time to time, whether on daily, weekly, or monthly basis, they meet with one another, sleep with one another, have intercourse, etc. Sometimes divorced women with careers also carry out this type of nikāḥ.

This type of *Nikāḥ* is becoming more and more prevalent in Saudi Arabia, and many young women are entering into this type of *Nikāḥ* there as some of their *shuyūkh* have allowed it. However, I disagree with this practice from a moral stance, for though it is legally ok, there are other aspects which we must consider beyond legality, such as its

[100] Hughes, Donna M. (2004) 'Sex Slave Jihad', (online) www.pezhvak.com.

impact on society and moral decency. Just as Ụmar bin al-Khaṭṭāb ﷺ disapproved of Ḥudhaifah bin al-Yamān ﷺ and others marrying *Ahl al-Kitāb* women despite its legality, so too is the case here.

One should perform the *rukhsatī* after the *Nikāḥ as soon as possible* and avoid any delays as this is best, and *Nikāḥ Misyār* should be avoided.

MARRYING WITH THE INTENTION OF DIVORCE

To marry someone with the intention that you will divorce them as soon as your needs are fulfilled is not right. This is a form of treachery and deception. So why deceive the other person? They are thinking that you are marrying them for life, whereas you are intending to divorce as soon as your need is fulfilled. This is not right.

Some people get married to people from the UK for the purpose of a visa or to gain nationality, and intend to leave them as soon as their purpose is achieved. These types of marriages are scams and not allowed. Avoid them.

CIVIL MARRIAGES

According to the law we have to provide paperwork for a civil marriage. However, you should have your Islamic *Nikāḥ* done first and then the civil marriage registration or ceremony later, because you want to do your *Nikāḥ* according to the *Sunnah*. If the civil marriage is done first, it would be the same as conducting nikāḥ, because there is proposal of acceptance in the presence of two male witnesses. Therefore, holding a separate *Nikāḥ* ceremony in the masjid will simply become a formality. If you have to, for some reason, do the civil marriage first, then make sure that wherever the civil marriage takes place there are no male witnesses in attendance. This will mean that the marriage will be binding legally, but according to *Sharīạh* it will not be classed as a *Nikāḥ*. This will allow you to have *Nikāḥ* done in the masjid according to the *Sunnah* way.

MARRIAGE OVER THE PHONE

This is a relatively recent issue which has arisen due to the advancement in technology. For example, the bride may be in the UK and the groom may have gone for *ụmrah* and met a Shaykh and asked him to do their *Nikāḥ*. And the Shaykh agrees, so they phone the UK and that Shaykh is put on speaker. Would this *Nikāḥ* be proper and take effect?

The answer is no, because during the process of *Ījāb* and *Qubūl*, *ittiḥād-e-majlis* [everyone being present in a single gathering] is a necessary element for the *Nikāḥ* to be considered as Islamically proper and correct, where everyone including the two official witnesses are physically present throughout the *Nikāḥ* ceremony. Yet in this case one person is in one country and the other is in another country, so the *majlis* is different.

Instead, what needs to happen to legitimise their marriage in this case is that the woman appoints a *wakīl* to represent her there in Saudi Arabia and act on her behalf in the process of *Ījāb* and *Qubūl*, while she can listen to the ceremony over the phone or observe it over some form of video conferencing or video call.

FORCED MARRIAGES

As has been discussed previously, forced marriages are completely wrong and should be avoided. They are cultural and have nothing to do with Islam.

SECRET MARRIAGES

Marrying in secret is wrong and should be avoided. Marriage should be open and publicly announced, as is clear from the hadīth:

أَعْلِنُوا هَذَا النِّكَاحَ وَاجْعَلُوهُ فِي الْمَسَاجِدِ وَاضْرِبُوا عَلَيْهِ بِالدُّفُوفِ[101] وَفِيْ رِوَايَةٍ وَاضْرِبُوا عَلَيْهِ بِالْغِرْبَالِ[102]

[101] Tirmidhī: 1089.

[102] Ibn Mājah: 1970.

Publicise this Nikāḥ, and hold it in the masjid, and beat the Duff for it, [and in another narration] beat the sieve for it.

If we start giving permission for secret *Nikāḥ*, boys and girls will get married without their parents' knowledge. This has happened in cases and lead to problems. In one case, a young lady fell in love with a colleague of hers at work and was lured by him into marrying in secret without the knowledge of her friends and family. What the man didn't tell her was that he was already married. They would meet together after work and behave as husband and wife, after which she would go home and behave as normal. This relationship with him continued for several months. In the meantime, her parents engaged her to someone else and she began to panic, too afraid and embarrassed to tell them of what she had already done. She kept the knowledge to herself until just a few days before her *Nikāḥ* was to take place, at which point, unable to conceal it any longer, she opened up and told her parents everything. They had booked a huge hall and invited hundreds of guests and spent much money on food and other arrangements. Everything had to be cancelled. What is more, upon looking into her secret husband's background, they learned that he was already married and had children as well. All of this was news to the young lady who realised she had been tricked and betrayed from the outset. When people engage in secret marriages, these types of things can happen and lives can be ruined.

Having said this, if someone does perform a secret marriage and all the requirements of *Nikāḥ* are met, i.e. *Ījāb*, *Qubūl*, witnesses, *mahr*, and *Walī*, the *Nikāḥ* will be valid.

WHAT IS MAHR?

Mahr is the specified and legally required 'dower' payment given by the groom or his family directly to the bride. It is a gift given to her because of all the sacrifice she has to make in leaving her parents and siblings, and leaving the comfort and safety of her family home to go and live with her husband.

In the beginning there was no fixed amount for *mahr*, something as little as one metal ring, a pair of sandals, or teaching a few *āyah* of the Qur'ān was sufficient, as can be seen in the following *aḥādīth*:

تَزَوَّجْ وَلَوْ بِخَاتَمٍ مِنْ حَدِيدٍ .

Marry, even with [a Mahr equal to] an iron ring. [103]

زَوَّجْنَاكَهَا بِمَا مَعَكَ مِنَ الْقُرْآنِ .

We have married her to you for [a Mahr equal to] what you know of the Qur'ān [by heart]. [104]

أَنَّ امْرَأَةً، مِنْ بَنِي فَزَارَةَ تَزَوَّجَتْ عَلَى نَعْلَيْنِ فَقَالَ رَسُولُ اللهِ ﷺ " أَرَضِيتِ مِنْ نَفْسِكِ وَمَالِكِ بِنَعْلَيْنِ " . قَالَتْ نَعَمْ . قَالَ فَأَجَازَهُ .

A woman from Banū Fazārah married for [the Mahr of] two sandals. So the Messenger of Allāh ﷺ said to her: 'Do you approve of [exchanging] yourself and your wealth for two sandals?' She said: 'Yes.' So he permitted it. [105]

However, slowly, slowly as time moved on, and the religion became more and more complete, a minimum amount was fixed. At a later occasion, *Rasūlullāh* ﷺ said:

لا يَنْكِحِ النِّسَاءَ إِلا الأَكْفَاءُ ، وَلا يُزَوِّجْهُنَّ إِلا الأَوْلِيَاءُ ، وَلا مَهْرَ دُونَ عَشْرِ دَرَاهِمَ .

Women should only marry those of compatible/equivalent status, they should not be given in marriage except by their Walī, and there is no Mahr less than ten dirhams. [106]

---

[103] Bukhārī: 5150.

[104] Bukhārī: 5135, 5871.

[105] Tirmidhī: 1113.

[106] Dāraqutnī; Bayhaqī; Ibn Khuzaimah; Abū Yaʿlā.

Ten *dirhams* is the equivalent of approximately one troy ounce of silver [0.9873 troy oz.] or its monetary value [currently £12-15]. *Mahr* should not be less than this amount. If one wants to give more than this, then there is the *mahr* which the Beloved Prophet ﷺ specified for his daughter, the Lady Fāṭima ؓ upon her marriage with Ạlī ؓ. Her *mahr*, which is known as *mahr al-faṭimī*, was 500 *dirhams*, which is the equivalent of approximately 50 troy ounces of silver [49.38570 troy oz.] or its monetary value [currently £636]. However, there is no maximum limit and any number agreed upon by both sides is permissible.

THE ROLE OF A WALĪ [GUARDIAN]

A *Walī* is someone who has authority or guardianship over another person, such as a father is the *Walī* over his children who are in his care and is authorised in conducting a marriage contract for them wherever he thinks best. A person can become a *Walī* either through familial relation [i.e. father, grandfather, brother, uncle, etc.] or authority [i.e. Imām, community leader, judge, king, etc.]. If there is no relative to take care of the minor, then the *Amīr* [leader] or *Qādhī* [judge] will be considered as the *Walī* and will be authorised to be their agent in concluding a marriage contract.

To be considered as a valid *Walī*, the person must be:

[1] Muslim (an adherent of Islam).
[2] '*Āqil* (of sound mind).
[3] *Bāligh* (have reached maturity).

Both men and women can be the *Walī*, as gender makes no difference here. Furthermore, there are also different ranks of *walāyah* [guardianship] according to the *fuqahā* [jurists]. According to them, the closest in relation firstly is the son, then father, then brother, then paternal uncle, and then grandfather. Vis-à-vis with female relatives.

There are the following *aḥādīth* which state that:

لاَ نِكَاحَ إِلاَّ بِوَلِيٍّ .

There is no marriage without the permission of a guardian. [107]

أَيُّمَا امْرَأَةٍ نُكِحَتْ بِغَيْرِ إِذْنِ وَلِيِّهَا فَنِكَاحُهَا

بَاطِلٌ فَنِكَاحُهَا بَاطِلٌ فَنِكَاحُهَا بَاطِلٌ .

Whichever woman married without the permission of her Walī her marriage is invalid. Her marriage is invalid. Her marriage is invalid. [108]

Many of the Imāms, such as Imām Shāfi'ī , Imām Aḥmad ibn Ḥanbal , and the Ṣāḥibain [Imām Abū Yūsuf and Imām Muḥammad ibn al-Ḥasan al-Shaybānī], for this reason state that Nikāḥ should not be performed without the presence of the Walī, and doing so will render it invalid. Imām Abū Ḥanīfa says that if a woman marries without a Walī then there will be two scenarios:

[1] If she has married in accordance to her *kuff* [someone of suitable equivalence and compatibility according to her status] and she received her *mahr-e-mithl* [the *mahr* which someone of her household usually receives] as well, then the Nikāḥ will be considered valid.

[2] If she has married someone who is not her *kuff* or she did not get her *mahr-e-mithl*, then Imām Abū Ḥanīfa's first opinion is that this Nikāḥ will be suspended upon the condition that if her Walī approves then it is valid, otherwise it is null. His second opinion is that it is null regardless and that the Walī should be brought in to re-conduct the Nikāḥ.

In this day and age, the Hanafī School gives legal precedence to the opinion of the Ṣāḥibain that a girl should not marry on her own in

---

[107] Tirmidhī: 1101; Abū Dāwūd: 2085; Ibn Mājah: 1954, 1955.
[108] Tirmidhī: 1102.

secret without her *Walī*. The *Walī* needs to be present and the *Nikāḥ* should be performed openly and meet the formalities.

Before representing the girl, a *Walī* should seek her permission first to act on her behalf according to her will. If a proposal has been made for her, then it should be presented to her and she should be asked whether she is happy to accept it or not. The girl, who we will assume is of a mature enough age to marry, will either be a *bākirah* [virgin] or a *thayyibah* [widow or divorcee]. If she is a virgin, she does not have to clearly say '*yes I agree*', but can just indicate or gesture that she is happy with the proposal. When *Rasūlullāh* ﷺ informed his daughter Lady Fāṭima رضي الله عنها that Ali رضي الله عنه was asking for her hand in marriage, and asked her for her response, she lowered her head and kept quiet. He [ﷺ] interpreted her silence as her assent. He came back to Ali رضي الله عنه and told him that his proposal had been accepted. This shows that when a girl is mature she should not be forced into accepting a marriage, even if the parents think it is a good match. As for a previously married woman, she has to verbally consent to the marriage for it to go ahead.

THE SUNNAH METHOD OF CONDUCTING THE NIKĀḤ

The *Imām* will conduct the *Nikāḥ* and deliver the *khuṭbah*, in which he will recite the following three *ayahs*:

يَا أَيُّهَا الَّذِيْنَ اٰمَنُوْا اتَّقُوا اللهَ حَقَّ تُقٰتِهٖ وَلَا تَمُوْتُنَّ اِلَّا وَاَنْتُمْ مُّسْلِمُوْنَ ۝

O you who believe, fear Allāh, as He should be feared, and let not yourself die save as Muslims.[109]

يَا أَيُّهَا النَّاسُ اتَّقُوْا رَبَّكُمُ الَّذِيْ خَلَقَكُمْ مِّنْ نَّفْسٍ وَّاحِدَةٍ وَّخَلَقَ

[109] Qur'ān 3:102.

مِنْهَا زَوْجَهَا وَبَثَّ مِنْهُمَا رِجَالًا كَثِيْرًا وَّنِسَاءً ج

وَاتَّقُوا اللهَ الَّذِيْ تَسَاءَلُوْنَ بِهٖ وَالْاَرْحَامَ ط اِنَّ اللهَ كَانَ عَلَيْكُمْ رَقِيْبًا ۝

O men, fear your Lord who created you from a single soul, and from it created its match, and spread many men and women from the two. Fear Allāh in whose name you ask each other (for your rights), and fear (the violation of the rights of) the womb-relations. Surely, Allāh is watchful over you.[110]

يٰاَيُّهَا الَّذِيْنَ اٰمَنُوْا اتَّقُوا اللهَ وَقُوْلُوْا قَوْلًا سَدِيْدًا ۝ يُصْلِحْ لَكُمْ اَعْمَالَكُمْ

وَيَغْفِرْ لَكُمْ ذُنُوْبَكُمْ ط وَمَنْ يُّطِعِ اللهَ وَرَسُوْلَهٗ فَقَدْ فَازَ فَوْزًا عَظِيْمًا ۝

O you who believe, fear Allāh, and speak in straightforward words. (If you do so), Allāh will correct your deeds for your benefit, and forgive your sins for you. Whoever obeys Allāh and His Messenger achieves a great success.[111]

These verses were recited by the Beloved Prophet ﷺ when he performed the *khuṭbah* for *Nikāḥ*, which makes it part of the *Sunnah* to do so. [112] We see in all three verses the words '*Ittaqū*', i.e. 'be mindful, be careful', appear. This is because the Beloved Prophet ﷺ wants to remind us and stress the importance of *taqwā* at the time of *Nikāḥ*. We are at the point of marriage embarking on the journey of a lifetime, and beginning a whole new chapter in our lives, so it is important to be mindful and careful of fulfilling Allāh's commands throughout it.

ANNOUNCING THE NIKĀḤ

It is *Sunnah* to announce the *Nikāḥ* and make it openly known. In fact, according to Imām Mālik ؒ announcing the *Nikāḥ* is *wājib*, and if it is not announced then the *Nikāḥ* is incomplete. At the least it should be common knowledge within your local community that you are getting married.

Another point worth noting here is that it is not necessary to print elaborate and expensive cards in order to publicise the wedding. If

---

[110] Qur'ān 4:1.

[111] Qur'ān 33:70-71.

[112] Tirmidhī: 1105.

you have lots of wealth and wish to spend it, that is fine, but a simple and modest wedding is far better and more blessed.

THE BEST TIME AND PLACE TO HAVE THE NIKĀḤ

The best place for *Nikāḥ* is in the masjid, as the Beloved Prophet ﷺ said:

أَعْلِنُوا هَذَا النِّكَاحَ وَاجْعَلُوهُ فِي الْمَسَاجِدِ.

Publicise this marriage, and hold it in the Masjid. [113]

Therefore you should try your best to have the *Nikāḥ* take place in the masjid so as to attain the blessings of the location (*makān*) and because *Nikāḥ* is a form of worship. [114] However, if due to some reason or necessity you are not able to do this, then there is nothing wrong with holding the *Nikāḥ* in a wedding hall or such either.

As regards to time, Ibn al-Humām al-Hanafī (d. 861 AH/1457 CE) and others have mentioned that it is recommended (*Mustaḥab*) to conduct the *Nikāḥ* on a Friday,[115] preferably between the *Aṣr* and *Maghrib ṣalāh* times. This is because of the blessedness of Friday, with the time between the *Aṣr* and *Maghrib* prayers being mentioned as especially blessed for the acceptance of prayers (*du'ā*), and the hope that a *Nikāḥ* conducted at such a time will also be blessed. If it cannot be conducted between the *Aṣr* and *Maghrib* prayers, then the next best time would be after the *Jumu'ạh* prayer since more people would likely be able to attend and therefore help to publicise the *Nikāḥ* further, as well as gain the added blessing of a larger congregational d*u'ā*.

Ultimately, *Nikāḥ* is a matter of convenience and so, provided it is done according to the *Sharī'ah*, any time that best suits both sides of the family and is most convenient for them is fine and the above is simply stating what is the most preferred time to hold the *Nikāḥ*.

---

113 Tirmidhī: 1089, 1090.

114 Mullāh Ạlī al-Qārī, *Mirqāt al-Mafātīḥ* vol. 6: p.217.

115 Ibn al Humām, *Fatḥ al-Qadīr* vol. 3: p. 189; Ibn Qudāmah, Al-*Mughnī* vol. 7: p. 64.

INVITING PEOPLE

It is good to invite close friends and family over for the *Nikāḥ* but it is not necessary. You shouldn't place a burden on those relatives or friends who live far away to attend, rather you can just inform them that the *Nikāḥ* is taking place and ask them to make *du'ā* for its success. Obviously, if they are able to travel and it is convenient for them, then there is nothing wrong with their coming.

FEEDING PEOPLE AT THE TIME OF NIKĀḤ

While inviting people and feeding them at the *Walīma* feast is from the *Sunnah*, according to the *fuqahā* feeding them at the *Nikāḥ* is not. However, it is permissible and we cannot say it is *ḥarām*. If the bride's side of the family would like to host a feast and call friends and family to attend, that is completely fine. But it should be remembered that the *Walīma* is the actual *Sunnah*, and that occurs *after* the *rukhsatī* and is hosted by the groom's family. If the bride's side of the family want to share in hosting the *Walīma* that is also fine.

RUKHSATĪ

The Beloved Prophet of Allāh ﷺ conducted the *rukhsatī* (wedding recessional/bride's departure) of his daughter, Lady Fāṭima ؓ, by sending her with Umme Ayman ؓ to Ali's ؓ house. On the other hand, for the Mother of the Believers, Lady 'Āishah's ؓ *rukhsatī*, the Beloved Prophet ﷺ came himself to her parents' house to return with her. What does this signify? It means that there are no strictures, conditions, or requirements for how the bride's departure from her parents' home to her spouse's house should be conducted. Indeed, there is great flexibility in regards to *rukhsatī*. All the conditions and customs built up around this act are non-Islamic traditions and practices and should be completely avoided.

JAHEZ

Similarly with regard to displaying the *jahez* (by *imāla*, from the Arabic *jahāz*), i.e. 'the paraphernalia, vestments, and furniture of every kind which a bride brings to her husband's house', [116] this also an un-Islamic custom and practice, completely unnecessary, and not part of the *rukhsatī*. Furthermore, if the father of the bride wishes to provide the *jahez* at a later date, providing as the need arises, there is nothing wrong with this either. Finally, it is customary in some places for the groom to demand certain items and place conditions on what he wants in jahez for the bride. This is also wrong and the bride's father should not be forced to buy anything.

HONEYMOON

Once the bride and groom reach their home, there should be a place prepared for them (a suitable room with privacy, food, and drink, etc.) where they can relax and be comfortable. In this day and age, people often go for a honeymoon for a week or two. Some scholars are very strict in this regard and argue against it, citing that it is an emulation of a non-Islamic custom. Personally, I think there is nothing wrong with this, so long as you do not have your honeymoon exactly as the non-Muslims do. For example, you could go for *ụmrah* if it is affordable and so you're honeymoon would become an act of worship performed together.

Having a honeymoon holiday for a week or two allows the couple to be away from all friends and family and spend time alone together, which helps to create and strengthen a bond between them. This is good for their marriage and future together. In fact, Pīr Ghulām Ḥabīb (d. 1410 AH/1989 CE) would actively encourage and recommend that newlyweds go for a honeymoon.

---

[116] Platts, J.T. (1884) *A Dictionary of Urdu, Classical Hindi, and English*. London: W.H. Allen & Co.

GREETING ONE ANOTHER

Upon entering into their living quarters the couple should greet one another with *Salām*.

SUPPLICATION AND OFFERING PRAYERS

You should pray two *rak'ạh* together of *ḥājah* (need) and *shukr* (gratitude). It is permissible to perform these two *rak'ạh* in congregation together as well, with the bride standing behind the husband and him leading her in *ṣalāh*. After the *ṣalāh*, you can supplicate together and ask Allāh ﷻ for His help to keep your bond strong, bless your marriage, and help it to survive.

عَنْ أَبِي سَعِيدٍ ، مَوْلَى بَنِي قَالَ : تَزَوَّجْتُ امْرَأَةً ، وَأَنَا مَمْلُوكٌ ، فَدَعَوْتُ أَصْحَابَ النَّبِيِّ - صَلَّى اللهُ عَلَيْهِ وَسَلَّمَ - فِيهِمْ أَبُو ذَرٍّ، وَابْنُ مَسْعُودٍ، وَحُذَيْفَةُ، فَتَقَدَّمَ حُذَيْفَةُ لِيُصَلِّيَ بِهِمْ ، فَقَالَ أَبُو ذَرٍّ ، أَوْ رَجُلٌ : لَيْسَ لَكَ ذَلِكَ ، فَقَدَّمُونِي ، وَأَنَا مَمْلُوكٌ ، فَأَمَمْتُهُمْ فَعَلَّمُونِي قَالُوا : " إِذَا أُدْخِلَ عَلَيْكَ أَهْلُكَ فَصَلِّ رَكْعَتَيْنِ ، وَمُرْهَا فَلْتُصَلِّ خَلْفَكَ ، وَخُذْ بِنَاصِيَتِهَا ، وَسَلِ اللهَ خَيْرًا ، وَتَعَوَّذْ بِاللهِ مِنْ شَرِّهَا، ثُمَّ شَأْنَكَ وَشَأْنَ أَهْلِكَ.

It was narrated that Abū Sa'īd, the freed slave of Abū Usayd, said: I got married when I was a slave, and I invited some of the Companions of the Prophet (ﷺ), among whom were Ibn Mas'ūd, Abū Dhar and Ḥudhaifah . . . And they taught me and said: When your wife enters upon you, pray two rak'ạh and tell her to pray behind you, then place your hand on her head and ask Allāh, may He be exalted, for the good of what has entered upon you and seek refuge with Him from its evil, then go ahead and approach your wife. [117]

---

[117] Muṣannaf Ibn Abi Shaybah; Muṣannaf Ạbd al-Razzāq: 10462.

عَنْ أَبِي وَائِلٍ قَالَ : جَاءَ رَجُلٌ مِنْ بَجِيلَةَ إِلَى عَبْدِ الله ، فَقَالَ : إِنِّي قَدْ تَزَوَّجْتُ جَارِيَةً بِكْرًا ، وَإِنِّي قَدْ خَشِيتُ أَنْ تَفْرِكَنِي ، فَقَالَ عَبْدُ الله : إِنَّ الْإِلْفَ مِنَ الله ، وَإِنَّ الْفَرْكَ مِنَ الشَّيْطَانِ ، لِيُكَرِّهَ إِلَيْهِ مَا أَحَلَّ الله لَهُ، فَإِذَا أُدْخِلَتْ عَلَيْكَ فَمُرْهَا فَلْتُصَلِّ خَلْفَكَ رَكْعَتَيْنِ.

A man came to Ạbdullāh [Ibn Mas'ūd] ﷺ and said: I have gotten married to a young girl and I am afraid that she will dislike me. Ạbdullāh ﷺ said: Love is from Allāh and dislike is from the Shaytān, who wants to make hateful to you that which Allāh has permitted to you. So when she comes to you, tell her to pray two rak'ạh behind you. [118]

As for what *du'ās* you should supplicate, the following are mentioned within the *aḥādīth*:

اللّٰهُمَّ إِنِّي أَسْأَلُكَ خَيْرَهَا وَخَيْرَ مَا جَبَلْتَهَا عَلَيْهِ
وَأَعُوذُ بِكَ مِنْ شَرِّهَا وَمِنْ شَرِّ مَا جَبَلْتَهَا عَلَيْهِ.

O Allāh, I ask You for the good in her, and in the disposition You have given her; I take refuge in You from the evil in her, and in the disposition You have given her. [119]

اللّٰهُمَّ إِنِّي أَسْأَلُكَ مِنْ خَيْرِهَا وَخَيْرِ مَا جُبِلَتْ
عَلَيْهِ وَأَعُوذُ بِكَ مِنْ شَرِّهَا وَشَرِّ مَا جُبِلَتْ عَلَيْهِ .

O Allāh, I ask You for the goodness within her and the goodness which is placed within her nature. And I seek refuge with You from the evil which is placed within her nature. [120]

اللّٰهُمَّ ، بَارِكْ لِي فِي أَهْلِي ، وَبَارِكْ لَهُمْ فِيَّ ، وَارْزُقْنِي مِنْهُمْ ، وَارْزُقْهُمْ

---

[118] Mu'jam Awsaṭ Tabrānī: 4150; Muṣannaf Ạbd al-Razzāq: 10460-10461.

[119] Abū Dāwūd: 2160; Ibn Mājah: 2337.

[120] Ibn Mājah: 1993.

مِنِّي ، اللّٰهُمَّ اجْمَعْ بَيْنَنَا مَا جَمَعْتَ إِلَى خَيْرٍ ، وَفَرِّقْ بَيْنَنَا إِذَا فَرَّقْتَ إِلَى خَيْرٍ .

O Allāh, make my wife blessed for me and make me blessed for her. O Allāh! Give me sustenance from her and give her sustenance from me. O Allāh, unite us in the way You unite on what is good, and if You separate us, separate us on what is good. [121]

FOREPLAY

Before joining in sexual intercourse, it is important and necessary to first engage in foreplay to prepare yourselves. According to Anas bin Mālik ﵁, the Messenger of Allāh ﷺ is reported to have said:

لا يَقَعَنَّ أحدُكم على امرأتِه كما تَقَعُ البَهيمةُ وليكنْ بينهما رسولٌ قيل: وما الرسولُ ؟ قال: القُبْلَةُ والكَلامُ.

One should not fulfil one's (sexual) need from one's wife like an animal, rather there should be a message bearer between them. Someone asked: 'What is a message bearer?' He replied, 'Talking and Kissing.' [122]

A good and comprehensive book on this matter, to help those who are married, is Mufti Muḥammad bin Ādam al-Kawtharī's *Islamic Guide to Sexual Relations*.

SEXUAL RELATIONS

Sexual relations are one of the bounties and gifts from Allāh ﷻ, so we should be thankful to Allāh ﷻ and make du'ā. Layth bin Sạ'd (d. 174 AH/791 CE) would make du'ā before going to his wife. Umar would say that I have sexual relations with the intention that Allāh ﷻ blesses me a good child who does the *dhikr* of Allāh ﷻ, so I may be rewarded for every *Subḥān-Allāh* that child says. Indeed Allāh ﷻ states:

نِسَآؤُكُمْ حَرْثٌ لَّكُمْ ص فَأْتُوْا حَرْثَكُمْ اَنّٰى شِئْتُمْ ز

---

[121] Mụ'jam Awsaṭ Tabrānī: 4150; Muṣannaf Ạbd al-Razzāq: 10460-10461.

[122] Musnad al-Firdaws Dailamī 2: 55.

وَقَدِّمُوْا لِاَنْفُسِكُمْ ط وَاتَّقُوا اللّٰهَ وَاعْلَمُوْآ اَنَّكُمْ مُّلٰقُوْهُ ط وَبَشِّرِ الْمُؤْمِنِيْنَ ۝

Your women are tillage for you to cultivate. So, come to your tillage from where you wish, and advance something for yourselves, and fear Allāh, and know that you are to meet Him, and give good news to the believers. [123]

This verse tells us to have sexual relations with our spouses in whatever way we want and to send forth good, meaning try for some offspring. Those children can survive after you, *Inshāllāh*, and worship Allāh ﷻ and so become a means of reward for you even after your death.

Secondly, we have to remember that in sexual intercourse with your spouse there is the reward (*thawāb*) of *ṣadaqah* (alms/charity):

أَوَلَيْسَ قَدْ جَعَلَ اللهُ لَكُمْ مَا تَصَّدَّقُونَ إِنَّ بِكُلِّ تَسْبِيحَةٍ صَدَقَةً وَكُلِّ تَكْبِيرَةٍ صَدَقَةٌ وَكُلِّ تَحْمِيدَةٍ صَدَقَةٌ وَكُلِّ تَهْلِيلَةٍ صَدَقَةٌ وَأَمْرٌ بِالْمَعْرُوفِ صَدَقَةٌ وَنَهْىٌ عَنْ مُنْكَرٍ صَدَقَةٌ وَفِي بُضْعِ أَحَدِكُمْ صَدَقَةٌ " . قَالُوا يَا رَسُولَ اللهِ أَيَأْتِي أَحَدُنَا شَهْوَتَهُ وَيَكُونُ لَهُ فِيهَا أَجْرٌ قَالَ أَرَأَيْتُمْ لَوْ وَضَعَهَا فِي حَرَامٍ أَكَانَ عَلَيْهِ فِيهَا وِزْرٌ فَكَذَلِكَ إِذَا وَضَعَهَا فِي الْحَلاَلِ كَانَ لَهُ أَجْرٌ.

Has Allāh not prescribed for you (a course) by following which you can (also) do ṣadaqah? In every tasbīḥ (Subḥān-Allāh) there is a ṣadaqah; and every takbīr (Allāh-u-Akbar) is a ṣadaqah; and every taḥmīd (Alhamdulillāh) is a ṣadaqah; and every tahlīl (Lā-Ilāha-Ill-Allāh) is a ṣadaqah; and the enjoining of good is a ṣadaqah, and the forbidding of that which is evil is a ṣadaqah; and in man's sexual intercourse (with his wife) there is a ṣadaqah. They (the Companions) said: O Messenger of Allāh, is there reward for him who satisfies his sexual passion among us? He said: Tell me, if he were to devote it to something forbidden, would it

[123] Qur'ān 2:223.

not be a sin on his part? Similarly, if he were to devote it to something lawful, he should have a reward. [124]

Shaykh Ḥussain Aḥmad Madanī (d. 1376 AH/1957 CE) would say that a person's heart is cleansed through sexual union as it purifies the heart and cleanses the spirit, quoting Qāḍī 'Iyāḍ (d. 554 AH/1149 CE) as saying, 'Every lust blackens the heart, but the act of Halāl sexual union is one that enlightens it.' [125] This clearing of the heart and mind of all *waswasa* (satanic whispers) is why in the *Ḥadīth* of the Friday prayer it is stated:

مَنْ غَسَّلَ وَاغْتَسَلَ وَغَدَا وَابْتَكَرَ وَدَنَا مِنَ الإِمَامِ
وَلَمْ يَلْغُ كَانَ لَهُ بِكُلِّ خُطْوَةٍ عَمَلُ سَنَةٍ صِيَامُهَا وَقِيَامُهَا .

Whosoever has a bath and makes his wife have a bath, comes early to the masjid and sits near the imam, and does not engage in idle talk, he will have for every step he takes (the reward of) a year's worth of good deeds, (equivalent to) fasting and praying qiyām during it. [126]

The phrasing of having a bath and making your wife have a bath before coming for the Friday prayers is an indication towards having sexual intercourse. This is because if you have intercourse with your wife before coming for the *Jumu'ạh* prayer your mind will be clear of evil thoughts and you will be able to better concentrate in your *ịbādah* (worship). So, you should have intercourse with the intention of clearing your mind as well as fulfilling the needs of yourself and your spouse.

ETIQUETTES OF SEXUAL RELATIONS

Another point to remember, and one of the etiquettes of sexual relations, is that at the time of intercourse you should try to keep

---

[124] Muslim: 1006; Musnad Aḥmad: 20905, 20944.

[125] Nadwī, M.Z. (1982) *Modesty and Chastity in Islam*. Tr. Sharif Ahmad Khan. Kuwait: Islamic Book Publishers.

[126] Tirmidhī: 496; Abū Dāwūd: 345; Nasa'ī: 1392, 1395, 1409; Ibn Mājah: 1140.

yourselves covered. As well as this, you should try to ensure that you do not face towards the direction of the *Qiblah* during the act.

At the time of intercourse there is a special du'ā to pray that is related in numerous *aḥādīth*:

لَوْ أَنَّ أَحَدَكُمْ إِذَا أَرَادَ أَنْ يَأْتِيَ أَهْلَهُ فَقَالَ بِاسْمِ اللهِ، اللَّهُمَّ جَنِّبْنَا الشَّيْطَانَ، وَجَنِّبِ الشَّيْطَانَ مَا رَزَقْتَنَا. فَإِنَّهُ إِنْ يُقَدَّرْ بَيْنَهُمَا وَلَدٌ فِي ذَلِكَ لَمْ يَضُرَّهُ شَيْطَانٌ أَبَدًا.

If anyone of you, when having sexual relation with his wife, says: 'In the name of Allāh. O Allāh, protect us from Shayṭān and prevent Shayṭān from approaching the offspring you grant us,' and if it is destined that they should have a child then, Shayṭān will never be able to harm that offspring. [127]

Preferably this supplication should be made before uncovering. Also, there should be no shouting or screaming while your needs are being fulfilled. The *Sharī'ah* doesn't interfere with the manner in which you fulfil your need and that is left to the discretion of the couple, but the general manner can be ascertained from the following:

فَلَمَّا تَغَشَّاهَا حَمَلَتْ حَمْلًا خَفِيفًا فَمَرَّتْ بِهِ ۖ

So when he covers her with himself, she carries a light burden and moves about with it. [128]

إِذَا قَعَدَ بَيْنَ شُعَبِهَا الأَرْبَعِ وَأَلْزَقَ الْخِتَانَ بِالْخِتَانِ (وَفِي رِوَايَةٍ ثُمَّ اجْتَهَدَ) فَقَدْ وَجَبَ الْغُسْلُ .

[127] Bukhārī: 141, 3271, 5165, 6388, 7396; Muslim: 1434 a; Tirmidhī: 1092; Abū Dāwūd: 2161.

[128] Qur'ān 7:189.

When (a man) sits between the four parts of his wife's body and the parts (of the male and female) which are circumcised join together (and they exert themselves), then a bath becomes obligatory. [129]

The Qur'ān states:

نِسَآؤُكُمْ حَرْثٌ لَّكُمْ ص فَاْتُوْا حَرْثَكُمْ اَنّٰى شِئْتُمْ ز
وَقَدِّمُوْا لِاَنْفُسِكُمْ ط وَاتَّقُوا اللهَ وَاعْلَمُوْآ اَنَّكُمْ مُّلٰقُوْهُ ط وَبَشِّرِ الْمُؤْمِنِيْنَ ۝

Your women are tillage for you to cultivate. So, come to your tillage from where you wish, and advance something for yourselves, and fear Allāh, and know that you are to meet Him, and give good news to the believers. [130]

The *tafāsīr* (exegeses) explain this to mean whichever way you wish whether standing up, sitting down, lying down, from the front, or the back, as long as you avoid penetrating in the anus or during their menstruation, and quote the Companion Ạbdullāh bin Kạ'b ﵁ as mentioning such. [131]

Anal intercourse and intercourse during menstruation are both *ḥarām* (unlawful) and major sins. It is reported, that the Beloved Prophet ﷺ stated:

إِنْ شَاءَ مُجَبِّيَةً وَإِنْ شَاءَ غَيْرَ مُجَبِّيَةٍ غَيْرَ أَنَّ ذَلِكَ فِي صِمَامٍ وَاحِدٍ.

If he likes he may (have intercourse) being on the back or in front of her, but it should be through one opening (vagina). [132]

Also, when a person fulfils his desire, he should not stop immediately but rather continue until their partner's desire is also fulfilled. Secondly, once the act is completed there should be something kept at hand to clean themselves immediately in the aftermath. If you can do *ghusl* (bath) immediately, it is better to do so, otherwise you should

---

[129] Abū Dāwūd: 216; Nasa'ī: 193.

[130] Qur'ān 2:223.

[131] Tafsīr al-Jalālayn; Jāmị' al-Bayān (Ṭabarī).

[132] Muslim: 1435c.

perform *wudhū'* (ablution) and wash your private parts before going to sleep. If you cannot do so and delay it till the morning, this is also permissible. If you go to sleep and wake up a few hours later and desire to have sexual intercourse again, it is necessary to wash your private parts first before engaging.

Finally, it is from the etiquettes of sexual relations that whatever happens in the bedroom should not be discussed in front of other people. This is cited as a great breach of trust in the *aḥādīth.*

FREQUENCY OF SEXUAL RELATIONS

How often can you engage in sexual relations? Whenever the need arises and you feel it is necessary to do so. However, you also need to be mindful of your health and your partner as well.

A woman came to Ụmar ﷺ and said, 'My husband stands at night [in prayer] and fasts during the day.' Ụmar ﷺ said, 'You have praised your husband excellently well.' Kạ'b ibn Sawwar ﷺ said to Ụmar ﷺ, 'She is [actually] complaining.' Ụmar ﷺ asked, 'How so?' He said, 'She claims to have no share in the marriage from her husband [i.e. her husband does not fulfil her rights].' Ụmar ﷺ said, 'If you understand this much, then you decide between them.' He (Kạ'b) said, 'O *Amīr al-Mu'minīn*, Allāh has permitted him four wives. So she has one day of every four days, and one night of every four nights.' [133] And this is moderate path in regards to this matter.

Otherwise, as far as *Fardh* (obligation) is concerned, according to Imām Abū Hanīfā ﷺ only one act of sexual intercourse is necessary after marriage and the obligation will be complete. This is because according to Imām Abū Hanīfā ﷺ, if after the *Nikāḥ* a person cannot sleep with his wife even once then that is grounds for a divorce. If he does fulfil her needs once but then neglects her he will be considered very sinful. One should be considerate of his wife, and should not berate or rebuke her, accusing her of shamelessness if she asks for sex. It is her right to do so just as much as it is the husband's, and it is incumbent upon him to fulfil her needs. Similarly, unless the wife has

---

[133] Muṣannaf Ạbd al-Razzāq: 12586, 12587.

a religious reason (menstruation) or medical reason (illness) for refusing, she should not deny her husband when he calls her to bed. The Mother of the Believers Lady Umm Salamah ﵂ is reported to have said that if the wives of the Blessed Prophet ﷺ had a headache then he ﷺ would not disturb them.

MOST APPROPRIATE TIME FOR SEXUAL RELATIONS

Imām Ghazālī ﵀ (d. 504 AH/1111 CE) is of the opinion that the most appropriate time for intercourse is in the morning. This is because in the evening both parties may be weary or tired from the days chores, and may not have the energy to engage with each other. The usual habit of the Beloved Prophet ﷺ was to go to his wives and fulfil his need after praying *Tahajjud* and then bathing and going to the *masjid* for *Fajr*.

GHUSL (BATHING) AFTER INTERCOURSE

There are three *farāidh* in *ghusl*:

[1] To wash and gargle the mouth with water.
[2] To wash the inside of the nostrils all the way to the soft part of the base of nose.
[3] To wash the entire body once from head to toe, leaving no part dry.

Often times the brides have spent a lot of money to have their hair styled and conditioned and set for their wedding, so even after their first night with their husbands they try to preserve their hairstyle by wearing a shower cap when performing *ghusl*. In such a case, the *ghusl* is not complete because the hair has been left dry, whereas it must be washed. Similarly, all make up and nail varnish will have to be removed in order to complete the *ghusl*, and cannot be preserved regardless of how expensive it was to get done. Instead of nail varnish, *mehndi* (Henna) should be used, as the water reaches the nails beneath it.

THE TIME OF WALĪMA [MARRIAGE BANQUET]

Normally, we say that the time of the *Walīma* is after the *rukhsatī*, after the marriage has been consummated. However, Shaykh Rashīd Aḥmed Gangohī ﷺ (d. 1323 AH/1905 CE) says that when the bride comes to her new house, whatever food is fed, can be classed as a *Walīma* as well. The significance of this is that the *Walīma* can take place on the same day as well.

HOW MANY DAYS SHOULD THE WALĪMA LAST FOR ?

One day is preferred, although Imām Mālik ﷺ is of the opinion that a *Walīma* can stretch out over three to seven days, provided that the people who eat on each day are different. In this way many people can be covered. This could be a good solution for people who don't want to waste money booking an expensive hall, as in this way a great many people can be fed in the house if need be. However, there is a *hadīth* which states that:

الْوَلِيمَةُ أَوَّلُ يَوْمٍ حَقٌّ وَالثَّانِي مَعْرُوفٌ وَالْيَوْمُ الثَّالِثُ سُمْعَةٌ وَرِيَاءٌ.

The wedding feast on the first day is a duty, that on the second is a good practice, but that on the third day is to make men hear of it and hypocrisy (affected superiority and boastfulness). [134]

This is in the case where, rather than expediency, the whole purpose is to show off their wealth through excess. And this is the reason why there are *aḥādīth* which report:

شَرُّ الطَّعَامِ طَعَامُ الْوَلِيمَةِ يُدْعَى إِلَيْهِ الأَغْنِيَاءُ وَيُتْرَكُ الْمَسَاكِينُ.

[134] Abū Dāwūd: 3745.

The worst food is the food of the wedding feast to which the rich are invited and the poor are ignored. [135]

This is where particular care is made to invite the people who will give a big, fat envelope (money), and those known for only giving a small envelope are ignored.

HOW LONG SHOULD THE DURATION BE BETWEEN THE NIKĀḤ AND WALĪMA ?

As mentioned previously, it is highly preferable to have all events take place quickly and avoid any delays. Long durations between *Nikāḥ*, *Walīma*, and *Rukhsatī* should be avoided as such occurrences can cause trouble. Moreover, it is contrary to the *Sunnah*.

The Prophet ﷺ was the *Uswā-e-Ḥasanah* (the most excellent model of conduct) and so he left examples of how the *Walīma* should take place for both the rich and the poor. The *Walīma* feast given for the Mother of the Believers Lady Zainab bint Jaḥsh ﵅ is a beautiful model for those with wealth. Anas ﵁ states, 'I did not see the Prophet (ﷺ) giving a better banquet on marrying any of his wives than the one he gave on marrying Zainab ﵅, whereupon he gave a banquet of a whole goat.' [136] In another narration, Anas ﵁ states, 'When Allāh's Messenger (ﷺ) married Zainab bint Jaḥsh ﵅, he made the people eat meat and bread to their fill (by giving a *Walīma* banquet)'. [137] This is explained further, that 'He fed them bread and meat (so lavishly) that they (the guests) abandoned it (of their own accord after having taken them to their hearts' content)'.[138] Furthermore, Anas ﵁ explains how the Beloved Prophet ﷺ sent him out to invite more and more guests to the feast:

---

[135] Muwatta: 1145; Bukhārī: 5177; Muslim: 1432a, 1432b, 1432c, 1432d; Abū Dāwūd: 3742; Ibn Mājah: 1988.

[136] Bukhārī: 5168, 5171; Muslim: 1428c, 1428d; Abū Dāwūd: 3743; Ibn Mājah: 1983.

[137] Bukhārī: 4794; Muslim: 1428a.

[138] Muslim: 1428d.

عَنْ أَنَسٍ قَالَ بُنِيَ عَلَى النَّبِيِّ ﷺ بِزَيْنَبَ ابْنَةِ جَحْشٍ بِخُبْزٍ وَلَحْمٍ فَأُرْسِلْتُ عَلَى الطَّعَامِ دَاعِيًا فَيَجِيءُ قَوْمٌ فَيَأْكُلُونَ وَيَخْرُجُونَ، ثُمَّ يَجِيءُ قَوْمٌ فَيَأْكُلُونَ وَيَخْرُجُونَ، فَدَعَوْتُ حَتَّى مَا أَجِدُ أَحَدًا أَدْعُو فَقُلْتُ يَا نَبِيَّ اللهِ مَا أَجِدُ أَحَدًا أَدْعُوهُ قَالَ ارْفَعُوا طَعَامَكُمْ.

A banquet of bread and meat was held on the occasion of the marriage of the Prophet ﷺ to Zainab bint Jaḥsh. I was sent to invite the people (to the banquet), and so the people started coming (in groups). They would eat and then leave. Another batch would come, eat, and leave. So I kept on inviting the people till I found nobody to invite. Then I said, 'O Prophet of Allāh, I cannot find anybody else to invite. He said, 'Carry away with the remaining food.' [139]

As for those of us with less wealth, we have the example of the *Walīma* feast given in honour of the Mother of the Believers, Lady Ṣafīya bint Ḥuyai ﷺ. It was the *Sunnah* of the Beloved Prophet ﷺ that after victory in a battle, he would remain in that area for three days or more, and so was the case with *Khaybar*. It was there that the Beloved Prophet ﷺ married Lady Ṣafīya ﷺ:

عَنْ أَنَسٍ، قَالَ أَقَامَ النَّبِيُّ ﷺ بَيْنَ خَيْبَرَ وَالْمَدِينَةِ ثَلاَثًا يُبْنَى عَلَيْهِ بِصَفِيَّةَ بِنْتِ حُيَىٍّ فَدَعَوْتُ الْمُسْلِمِينَ إِلَى وَلِيمَتِهِ، فَمَا كَانَ فِيهَا مِنْ خُبْزٍ وَلاَ لَحْمٍ، أَمَرَ بِالأَنْطَاعِ فَأُلْقِيَ فِيهَا مِنَ التَّمْرِ وَالأَقِطِ وَالسَّمْنِ فَكَانَتْ وَلِيمَتَهُ،

Anas ﷺ narrates that, 'The Prophet ﷺ stayed for three days at a place between Khaybar and Madīnah, and there he consummated his marriage with Ṣafīya bint Ḥuyai ﷺ. I invited the Muslims to a banquet which included neither meat nor bread. The Prophet ﷺ ordered for the leather dining sheets to be spread, and then dates, dried cheese and butter were provided over it, and that was the Walīma (banquet) of the Prophet ﷺ.' [140]

---

[139] Bukhārī: 4793.

[140] Bukhārī: 4213, 5085, 5159; Nasa'ī: 3382.

As the marriage and *Walīma* occurred on a journey, there was nothing close to hand with which to provide food. Therefore the Beloved Prophet ﷺ asked his companions to bring whatever of their rations they could, and that was the *Walīma* feast:

فَأَصْبَحَ النَّبِيُّ ﷺ عَرُوسًا فقَالَ " مَنْ كَانَ عِنْدَهُ شَيْءٌ فَلْيَجِئْ بِهِ " . وَبَسَطَ نِطَعًا، فَجَعَلَ الرَّجُلُ يَجِيءُ بِالتَّمْرِ، وَجَعَلَ الرَّجُلُ يَجِيءُ بِالسَّمْنِ ـ قَالَ وَأَحْسِبُهُ قَدْ ذَكَرَ السَّوِيقَ ـ قَالَ فَحَاسُوا حَيْسًا، فَكَانَتْ وَلِيمَةَ رَسُولِ اللهِ ﷺ .

So the Prophet ﷺ was a bridegroom and he said, 'Whoever has anything (food) should bring it.' He spread out a leather sheet (for the food) and some brought dates and others cooking butter. (I think he [Anas] mentioned As-Sawīq). So they prepared a dish of Ḥays (a kind of meal). And that was Walīma (the marriage banquet) of Allāh's Messenger ﷺ.[141]

فَلَمَّا أَصْبَحَ قَالَ رَسُولُ اللهِ صلى الله عليه وسلم " مَنْ كَانَ عِنْدَهُ فَضْلُ زَادٍ فَلْيَأْتِنَا بِهِ " . قَالَ فَجَعَلَ الرَّجُلُ يَجِيءُ بِفَضْلِ التَّمْرِ وَفَضْلِ السَّوِيقِ حَتَّى جَعَلُوا مِنْ ذَلِكَ سَوَادًا حَيْسًا فَجَعَلُوا يَأْكُلُونَ مِنْ ذَلِكَ الْحَيْسِ وَيَشْرَبُونَ مِنْ حِيَاضٍ إِلَى جَنْبِهِمْ مِنْ مَاءِ السَّمَاءِ - قَالَ - فَقَالَ أَنَسٌ فَكَانَتْ تِلْكَ وَلِيمَةَ رَسُولِ اللهِ ﷺ.

When it was morning Allāh's Messenger ﷺ said, 'He who has surplus of provision with him should bring that to us'. Some persons would bring surplus of dates, and the other surplus barley mush, until they made from it a black coloured Ḥays. They began to eat the Ḥays and began to drink from the water of a pond beside them, which had formed from rainfall. And that was the Walīma feast of Allāh's Messenger ﷺ.[142]

---

[141] Bukhārī: 371; Muslim: 1365c; Nasa'ī: 3380.

[142] Muslim: 1365f.

So, if you are in a situation of poverty and can't afford the expense of a *Walīma* feast, it is okay to ask neighbours and friends to help with the food and then invite people to the feast. *Rasūlullāh* ﷺ is the *Uswā-e-Ḥasanah* and his *Sunnah* is for everyone. A *Walīma* does not have to be huge or extravagant, with hundreds of guests and thousands of pounds spent. The Prophetic way is simple.

FEEDING AT THE TIME OF WALĪMA

This can take place at your house as well and does not necessitate booking an expensive wedding hall or function suite. In fact, one *hadīth* mentions that the Beloved Prophet ﷺ was a guest at one *Walīma* where the bride herself was serving the guests and served the Beloved Prophet ﷺ:

عَنْ أَبِي حَازِمٍ، قَالَ سَمِعْتُ سَهْلَ بْنَ سَعْدٍ، أَنَّ أَبَا أُسَيْدٍ السَّاعِدِيَّ، دَعَا النَّبِيَّ ﷺ لِعُرْسِهِ، فَكَانَتِ امْرَأَتُهُ خَادِمَهُمْ يَوْمَئِذٍ وَهْىَ الْعَرُوسُ. فَقَالَتْ أَوْ قَالَ أَتَدْرُونَ مَا أَنْقَعَتْ لِرَسُولِ اللهِ ﷺ أَنْقَعَتْ لَهُ تَمَرَاتٍ مِنَ اللَّيْلِ فِي تَوْرٍ.

Abū Usayd As-Sā'idī invited the Prophet ﷺ to his wedding banquet. At that time his wife was serving them, and she was the bride. She said (or Sahl said), 'Do you know what she soaked for Allāh's Messenger ﷺ? She soaked some dates for him (in water) in a drinking bowl overnight.' [143]

This demonstrates that a *Walīma* can be very simple, to the point where even the bride can help in the serving process.

INTERMINGLING OF OPPOSITE GENDERS DURING THE WALĪMA

[143] Bukhārī: 5183, 5597; Muslim: 2006a.

This – along with all the other issues that come along with it, such as photography and unnecessary video recording – should be avoided. Of course, in some countries or situations *it is* necessary in order to provide evidence of the marriage, such as if you are marrying outside of your own country of residence. Again, however, it must be stressed that if there is no necessity then it should be avoided.

MUSIC, SINGING AND DANCING

The rulings around music and dancing are quite clear cut and require no extensive explanation. With regards to singing at a wedding feast, if it is without musical instrumentation and without violating the rulings of *ḥijāb*, it may be allowed to a certain extent. If, for example, one plays *nasheeds* about marriage on the speaker system, then there is nothing wrong with this as long as there is no music involved. Sometimes in the *Walīma* hall you may need to play some *nasheeds* as without something to occupy the guests, they may make a great deal of noise. Moreover, such entertainment is established from the *Sunnah*. When the Beloved Prophet ﷺ came to Madīnah, the culture of Madīnah was very different from the culture of Makkah. The people of Makkah were very simple and straightforward, while the people of Madīnah had certain cultural customs during weddings and so forth. One girl from the *Anṣār* was an orphan and was fostered by Lady Ā'ishah ﵂, who also arranged her wedding:

عَنْ عَائِشَةَ، أَنَّهَا زَفَّتِ امْرَأَةً إِلَى رَجُلٍ مِنَ الأَنْصَارِ فَقَالَ نَبِيُّ اللهِ ﷺ

"يَا عَائِشَةُ مَا كَانَ مَعَكُمْ لَهْوٌ فَإِنَّ الأَنْصَارَ يُعْجِبُهُمُ اللَّهْوُ".

The Mother of the Believers, Lady 'Ā'ishah ﵂ narrates that she prepared a lady for marriage to a man from the Anṣār when the Prophet ﷺ asked, 'O 'Ā'ishah, have you arranged any entertainment (during the marriage ceremony), as the Anṣār do like amusement?' [144]

---

[144] Bukhārī: 5162.

عَنِ ابْنِ عَبَّاسٍ، قَالَ أَنْكَحَتْ عَائِشَةُ ذَاتَ قَرَابَةٍ لَهَا مِنَ الأَنْصَارِ فَجَاءَ رَسُولُ اللهِ ﷺ فَقَالَ " أَهْدَيْتُمُ الْفَتَاةَ " . قَالُوا نَعَمْ . قَالَ " أَرْسَلْتُمْ مَعَهَا مَنْ يُغَنِّي قَالَتْ لاَ . فَقَالَ رَسُولُ اللهِ ﷺ " إِنَّ الأَنْصَارَ قَوْمٌ فِيهِمْ غَزَلٌ فَلَوْ بَعَثْتُمْ مَعَهَا مَنْ يَقُولُ أَتَيْنَاكُمْ أَتَيْنَاكُمْ فَحَيَّانَا وَحَيَّاكُمْ .

Ibn Abbās ﵁ narrates that Lady 'Ā'ishah ﵂ arranged a marriage for a female relative of hers among the Anṣār. The Messenger of Allāh ﷺ came and said: 'Have you taken the girl (to her husband's house)?' They said, 'Yes.' He asked, 'Have you sent someone with her to sing?' 'No, (we haven't)' Lady 'Ā'ishah ﵂ replied. So the Messenger of Allāh ﷺ said, 'The Anṣār are a people of gallantry and romantic temperament. Why didn't you send someone with her to sing, "We have come to you, we have come to you, may Allāh bless you and us?"' [145]

The Beloved Prophet ﷺ had great love for the *Anṣār* and their ways, and often expressed this:

عَنْ أَنَسٍ، أَنَّ النَّبِيَّ ﷺ رَأَى صِبْيَانًا وَنِسَاءً مُقْبِلِينَ مِنْ عُرْسٍ فَقَامَ نَبِيُّ اللهِ ﷺ مُمْثِلاً - وَفِي رِوَايَةٍ مُمْتَنًّا - فَقَالَ "اللَّهُمَّ أَنْتُمْ مِنْ أَحَبِّ النَّاسِ إِلَيَّ اللَّهُمَّ أَنْتُمْ مِنْ أَحَبِّ النَّاسِ إِلَيَّ" . يَعْنِي الأَنْصَارَ .

Anas ﵁ reports that once the Prophet ﷺ saw some women and children (of the Anṣār) coming back from a wedding party. Allāh's Apostle ﷺ stood up motionless (as a mark of respect) and happily and said, 'O Allāh, (bear witness) (and addressing the Anṣār, said) you are dearest to me amongst all people.' And he meant the Anṣār ﵃. [146]

EXTRAVAGANCE VS SIMPLICITY

يٰبَنِيْٓ اٰدَمَ خُذُوْا زِيْنَتَكُمْ عِنْدَ كُلِّ مَسْجِدٍ وَّكُلُوْا

---

[145] Ibn Mājah: 1975.

[146] Bukhārī: 378s5, 5180; Muslim: 2508.

وَاشْرَبُوْا وَلَا تُسْرِفُوْا ج اِنَّهُ لَا يُحِبُّ الْمُسْرِفِيْنَ ۝

Eat and drink and do not be extravagant. Surely, He does not like the extravagant. [147]

وَلَا تُبَذِّرْ تَبْذِيْرًا ۝ اِنَّ الْمُبَذِّرِيْنَ كَانُوْٓا اِخْوَانَ الشَّيٰطِيْنِ ط وَكَانَ الشَّيْطٰنُ لِرَبِّهٖ كَفُوْرًا ۝

And do not squander recklessly. Surely, squanderers are brothers to the Satan, and the Satan is very ungrateful to his Lord. [148]

These verses make it very clear that simplicity should always be given preference over extravagance.

WHO SHOULD BE INVITED ?

From the *aḥādīth* it becomes clear that everyone with whom you associate should bẹ invited. Don't leave the poor out, strive to insure that they are invited as well. As a point, for my son Ahmed's wedding, I specifically strove to invite those people especially from amongst our community who are considered to be *fuqarā*.

THE RIGHTS AND RESPONSIBILITIES OF THE HUSBAND AND WIFE

أَلاَ وَاسْتَوْصُوا بِالنِّسَاءِ خَيْرًا فَإِنَّمَا هُنَّ عَوَانٌ عِنْدَكُمْ لَيْسَ تَمْلِكُونَ مِنْهُنَّ شَيْئًا غَيْرَ ذَلِكَ إِلاَّ أَنْ يَأْتِينَ بِفَاحِشَةٍ مُبَيِّنَةٍ فَإِنْ فَعَلْنَ فَاهْجُرُوهُنَّ فِي الْمَضَاجِعِ وَاضْرِبُوهُنَّ ضَرْبًا غَيْرَ مُبَرِّحٍ فَإِنْ أَطَعْنَكُمْ فَلاَ تَبْغُوا عَلَيْهِنَّ سَبِيلاً أَلاَ إِنَّ لَكُمْ عَلَى نِسَائِكُمْ حَقًّا وَلِنِسَائِكُمْ عَلَيْكُمْ حَقًّا فَأَمَّا حَقُّكُمْ

[147] Qur'ān 7:31.

[148] Qur'ān 17:26-27.

عَلَى نِسَائِكُمْ فَلاَ يُوطِئْنَ فُرُشَكُمْ مَنْ تَكْرَهُونَ وَلاَ يَأْذَنَّ فِي بُيُوتِكُمْ مَنْ
تَكْرَهُونَ أَلاَ وَإِنَّ حَقَّهُنَّ عَلَيْكُمْ أَنْ تُحْسِنُوا إِلَيْهِنَّ فِي كِسْوَتِهِنَّ وَطَعَامِهِنَّ.

Be good to women and treat them kindly, for they are as captives in your care, and you have no sovereignty over them beyond this unless they commit a clearly shameless act. If they do that, then leave them apart in beds and chastise them in a way which causes no hurt or anguish. Then, if they obey you, do not seek a way against them. Indeed you have rights over your women, and your women have rights over you. As for your rights over your women, then they must not allow anyone whom you dislike to treat on your bedding (furniture), nor to permit anyone whom you dislike in your homes. And their rights over you are that you treat them well in clothing them and feeding them. [149]

The rights and responsibilities of a husband towards his wife can be divided into two categories, *Shar'ịī* (legal) and *Akhlāqī* (ethical). As for the *Shar'ịī* responsibilities, they can be categorised into three different aspects. Firstly, he is responsible for providing her with *ḥalāl* food and provision, meaning it is his responsibility alone to go out and earn in a lawful manner. The wife does not have to go out and earn a living. Secondly, as the aforementioned *Ḥadīth* implies, he must provide her with clothing. This should be done within reason and limited to what is needed according to the custom of the society. In regard to this, the *Ḥadīth* mentions:

عَنْ حَكِيمِ بْنِ مُعَاوِيَةَ، عَنْ أَبِيهِ، أَنَّ رَجُلاً، سَأَلَ النَّبِيَّ ﷺ مَا حَقُّ الْمَرْأَةِ
عَلَى الزَّوْجِ قَالَ " أَنْ يُطْعِمَهَا إِذَا طَعِمَ وَأَنْ يَكْسُوَهَا إِذَا اكْتَسَى وَلاَ
يَضْرِبِ الْوَجْهَ وَلاَ يُقَبِّحْ وَلاَ يَهْجُرْ إِلاَّ فِي الْبَيْتِ".

A man asked the Prophet ﷺ, 'What are the rights of a woman over her husband?' He said, 'That he should feed her as he feeds himself, and clothe her as he clothes himself; he should not strike her on the face nor disfigure her, and he should not abandon her except in the house (as a form of discipline).' [150]

---

[149] Tirmidhī: 1163, 3367; Ibn Mājah: 1924.

[150] Ibn Mājah: 1923.

Excessiveness in buying clothing and accessorising for every outfit is a needless waste and should be avoided. Thirdly, the husband has a legal responsibility towards his wife to provide her with a means of shelter, lodging, or place of living. Again, as mentioned in previous chapters, if she has a private room within a house, then that is enough. She needs a private space away from the rest of the family, and if she is not given this and instead has to share her room with others, then this is a legitimate grievance and withholding of her rights. Finally, a husband also has a moral and ethical responsibility towards his wife as well. This is to do his utmost to protect her and safeguard her from all harm; to care for her health, safety, and well-being; and to help her progress spiritually and bring her closer to Allāh ﷻ.

Wives also bear responsibilities towards their husbands. First and foremost, the primary right of the husband which is stressed in a great number of *aḥādīth* is that the wife should come to his bed whenever he calls her, and that sexual relations should not be denied to him without a valid reason (such as menstruation, etc.). The Beloved Prophet ﷺ is reported to have said:

فَإِنِّي لَوْ كُنْتُ آمِرًا أَحَدًا أَنْ يَسْجُدَ لِغَيْرِ اللهِ لأَمَرْتُ الْمَرْأَةَ أَنْ تَسْجُدَ لِزَوْجِهَا وَالَّذِي نَفْسُ مُحَمَّدٍ بِيَدِهِ لاَ تُؤَدِّي الْمَرْأَةُ حَقَّ رَبِّهَا حَتَّى تُؤَدِّيَ حَقَّ زَوْجِهَا وَلَوْ سَأَلَهَا نَفْسَهَا وَهِيَ عَلَى قَتَبٍ لَمْ تَمْنَعْهُ.

If I were to command anyone to prostrate to anyone other than Allāh, I would have commanded women to prostrate to their husbands. By the One in Whose Hand is the soul of Muhammad (ﷺ)! No woman can fulfil her duty towards Allāh until she fulfils her duty towards her husband. If he asks her (for intimacy), even if she is on her camel saddle, she should not refuse. [151]

Her second duty is that whatever wealth or property her husband has should be guarded and looked after by her, and not wasted. She should not be rash in expending it, regardless of how much her husband

---

[151] Ibn Mājah: 1926.

earns. Both of these responsibilities are summed up in the following *aḥādīth:*

عَنْ أَبِي هُرَيْرَةَ، قَالَ قِيلَ لِرَسُولِ اللهِ ﷺ أَىُّ النِّسَاءِ خَيْرٌ قَالَ "الَّتِي تَسُرُّهُ إِذَا نَظَرَ وَتُطِيعُهُ إِذَا أَمَرَ وَلاَ تُخَالِفُهُ فِي نَفْسِهَا وَمَالِهَا بِمَا يَكْرَهُ ".

It was asked of the Messenger of Allāh ﷺ, 'Which woman is best?' He said, 'The one who makes him happy when he looks at her, obeys him when he commands her, and she does not go against his wishes with regard to herself nor her wealth.' [152]

وَعَنِ ابْنِ عَبَّاسٍ أَنَّ رَسُولَ اللهِ ﷺ قَالَ: أَرْبَعٌ مَنْ أُعْطِيهِنَّ فَقَدْ أُعْطِيَ خَيْرَ الدُّنْيَا وَالْآخِرَةِ: قَلْبٌ شَاكِرٌ ، وَلِسَانٌ ذَاكِرٌ ، وَبَدَنٌ عَلَى الْبَلَاءِ صَابِرٌ ، وَزَوْجَةٌ لَا تَبْغِيهِ خَوْنًا فِي نَفْسِهَا وَمَالِهِ.

It was narrated that Ibn Ābbās رضي الله عنهما said that the Messenger of Allāh ﷺ said, 'There are four things that whoever is bestowed them has been bestowed the best of the world and the hereafter. (They are) a grateful and contented heart, a tongue constant in dhikr (remembrance of Allāh), a body patient in the face of ordeals and afflictions, and a wife who is not unfaithful in regard to herself or his property.' [153]

خَيْرُ نِسَاءٍ رَكِبْنَ الإِبِلَ نِسَاءُ قُرَيْشٍ. وَقَالَ الآخَرُ صَالِحُ نِسَاءِ قُرَيْشٍ. أَحْنَاهُ عَلَى وَلَدٍ فِي صِغَرِهِ، وَأَرْعَاهُ عَلَى زَوْجٍ فِي ذَاتِ يَدِهِ.

Amongst all those women who ride camels (i.e. the Arabs), the righteous ladies of the Quraysh are the best. They are merciful and kind to their off-spring and the best guardians of their husbands' properties. [154]

أَلاَ أُخْبِرُكَ بِخَيْرِ مَا يَكْنِزُ الْمَرْءُ الْمَرْأَةُ الصَّالِحَةُ إِذَا نَظَرَ إِلَيْهَا

---

[152] Nasa'ī: 3231.

[153] Mishkāt al-Maṣābīḥ: 3273; Shu'ạbul Īmān (Baihaqī): 4113.

[154] Bukhārī: 3434, 5082, 5365; Muslim: 2527a, 2527c, 2527e.

سَرَّتْهُ وَإِذَا أَمَرَهَا أَطَاعَتْهُ وَإِذَا غَابَ عَنْهَا حَفِظَتْهُ.

Let me inform you about the best a man hoards; it is a virtuous woman who pleases him when he looks at her, obeys him when he gives her a command, and guards his interests when he is away from her. [155]

مَا اسْتَفَادَ الْمُؤْمِنُ بَعْدَ تَقْوَى اللهِ خَيْرًا لَهُ مِنْ زَوْجَةٍ صَالِحَةٍ إِنْ أَمَرَهَا أَطَاعَتْهُ وَإِنْ نَظَرَ إِلَيْهَا سَرَّتْهُ وَإِنْ أَقْسَمَ عَلَيْهَا أَبَرَّتْهُ وَإِنْ غَابَ عَنْهَا نَصَحَتْهُ فِي نَفْسِهَا وَمَالِهِ.

Nothing is of more benefit to the believer after the Taqwā of Allāh than a righteous wife whom, if he commands her she obeys him, if he looks at her he is pleased, if he swears an oath concerning her she fulfils it, and when he is away from her she is sincere towards him with regard to herself and his wealth. [156]

There was a man once who was quite ugly and who had the good fortune to marry an exceedingly beautiful woman. One day, he told his wife that they were both *Jannatī* (People of Heaven). 'How so?' she asked, surprised by the boldness of his claim. 'Whenever I look at you,' he said, 'I am enchanted by your beauty and overwhelmed by extreme gratitude to Allāh who has blessed me with you. And as you know, the grateful people shall enter heaven.' 'And what of me?' his wife teased, 'How can you be so sure that I will go to heaven?' 'Well, I am aware of the ugliness of my appearance, and I know on some days it must depress you to no end whenever you look at me. Yet you remain patient with what Allāh has granted you for a husband. And as you know, the patient will also enter heaven.'

A good husband or wife is the one who actively takes care and fulfils his or her responsibility. It should be noted that the question of 'rights' for the husband or wife only comes up when there are already some underlying issues. People today are quick to demand their own rights and feel privileged, whereas if everyone was concerned with fulfilling their own responsibilities to the other person there would

---

[155] Abū Dāwūd: 1664.

[156] Ibn Mājah: 1930.

never be any issues. In such a world, there would be no need to make demands. Be caring, sharing, and helpful to one another and you will see there will be no need to demand your rights. A marital relationship is not something which should be negotiated through in terms of legal legislation, but rather should be based on love, consent, and caring.

HOW OFTEN CAN THE WIFE VISIT HER PARENTS AND RELATIVES ?

The wife should seek to gain her husband's consent before going to visit her parent's house, and if he has given permission then it is okay. With regards to the *Shar'īī* (legal) ruling on this matter, Imām Ạbdullāh bin Muḥammad al-Mawṣilī ﷺ (d. 683 AH/1284 CE) states that:

The husband has a right to prevent his wife's family members from visiting her in his house (for the house belongs to him). However, he should not stop them from talking to her and seeing her (at any time, for that would be the severing of ties . . . It is said: He should not prevent her from visiting her parents, and another opinion states, he can do so). He cannot prevent her parents from visiting her once a week, and other family members once a year.[157]

According to Ạllāmah Ibn 'Ābidīn ﷺ (d. 1252 AH/1836 CE): The husband should not prevent his wife from leaving to visit her parents once a week if they are not able to visit her . . . It is related from Imām Abū Yūsuf ﷺ that her leaving to visit her parents is pre-conditional to them being unable to visit her.[158]

Another issue which should be taken into consideration in this matter is the timeframe. If she is newlywed and wants to visit her parents every day, let her do so. As she slowly becomes accustomed to her new life, and as time moves on, she herself will settle down and the visits will become infrequent. So, one should be extra considerate in this regard as well. Furthermore, in this day and age it is very easy

---

[157] Al-Ikhtiyār li Tạlīl al-Mukhtār: 3/228.

[158] Radd al-Mukhtār: 2/664.

for her to see and speak with her parents through the benefit of modern technology such as phones, WhatsApp, Skype, and other social media.

THE IN-LAWS

Imam Nawawī ﷺ (d. 676 AH/1277 CE) states that a bride is not obliged by the *Sharīạ* (Islamic Law) to serve her In-laws, however by *mu'āshirah* (common social or cultural practice) she is obliged to serve her In-laws.[159] The *Sharīạ* will not dictate this, and will only say that she has to fulfil certain rights of her husband, however cultural custom and social ethics dictate that she be nice to her In-laws and to treat them how she would want her own parents to be treated. Conversely, the In-laws should also be considerate. Sometimes the mother-in-law and father-in-law may be hale and healthy and capable of carrying out small tasks themselves, yet they will insist on asking their daughter-in-law to carry out even the smallest of tasks for them. Eventually, the mole hill becomes a mountain and the straw becomes a large bale of hay. Bring water, make tea, serve the guests, bring this, bring that, make this, and make that. She is not your slave; she is your daughter. In fact, you should treat her better than your daughter, as your daughter will go to live somewhere else while she will stay with you. Treat her how you would want your own daughter to be treated at her in-laws' house.

An excellent example of this is when the wives of the Beloved Prophet ﷺ asked his daughter, Lady Fāṭima ﷺ to make a request on their behalf in regards to the Mother of the Believers, Lady 'Ā'ishah ﷺ. The following exchange took place:

فَقَالَ لَهَا رَسُولُ الله ﷺ "أَىْ بُنَيَّةُ أَلَسْتِ تُحِبِّينَ مَنْ أُحِبُّ"

. قَالَتْ بَلَى . قَالَ "فَأَحِبِّي هَذِهِ" .

[159] Al Minhāj Bi-Sharḥ Ṣaḥīḥ Muslim.

Allah's Messenger ﷺ said to her (Fāṭima), 'O my daughter, don't you love the one whom I love?' She said, 'Yes, (I do).' Thereupon he said, 'Then you should love this one as well [i.e. 'Ā'ishah ﵂ who would be her step-mother].' [160]

Rasūlullāh ﷺ asked his daughter to show love and respect for her step-mother as he loved her. Similarly, daughters-in-law should show love and respect for their husbands' parents because their husbands love them. And the same principle applies to the parents, who should love and respect their daughters-in-law because their sons love them. The Lady Fāṭima ﵂ and the Mother of the Believers, Lady 'Ā'ishah ﵂ had much love for each other, even long after the passing of the Beloved Prophet ﷺ.

POLYGAMY

This is another difficult issue. One should remember that polygamy is neither a *Fardh* nor a *Sunnah* action, and will be regarded as something which is *mubāḥ* (permissible) if one is able to guarantee that they will be able to maintain fairness in dealing with their wives. Allāh ﷻ commands:

فَانْكِحُوْا مَا طَابَ لَكُمْ مِّنَ النِّسَاءِ مَثْنٰى وَثُلٰثَ وَرُبٰعَ ۚ
فَاِنْ خِفْتُمْ اَلَّا تَعْدِلُوْا فَوَاحِدَةً ۝

... Then, marry the women you like, in twos, in threes and in fours. But, if you fear that you will not maintain equity, then (keep to) one woman ...[161]

If you think you are capable of treating two, three, or four wives equally, then it is permissible to marry so. But one should also heed the following warning:

[160] Muslim: 2442a; Nasa'ī: 3944.

[161] Qur'ān 4:3.

مَنْ كَانَتْ لَهُ امْرَأَتَانِ فَمَالَ إِلَى إِحْدَاهُمَا جَاءَ يَوْمَ الْقِيَامَةِ وَشِقُّهُ مَائِلٌ.

Whosoever has two wives and inclines towards (favours) one of them (over the other), he will come on the Day of Resurrection with one of his sides leaning (i.e. half-paralysed). [162]

وَلَنْ تَسْتَطِيْعُوْٓا اَنْ تَعْدِلُوْا بَيْنَ النِّسَآءِ وَلَوْ حَرَصْتُمْ

فَلَا تَمِيْلُوْا كُلَّ الْمَيْلِ فَتَذَرُوْهَا كَالْمُعَلَّقَةِ ۝

You shall never be able to maintain real equality between wives, even though you are eager to (do so). So, do not lean totally (towards one) and leave the other as suspended. If you act righteously and fear Allāh, then, Allāh is Most-Forgiving, Very-Merciful. [163]

There are two things: one is the outer behaviour and equality and fairness in treatment, and the other is the inner matter of the love you feel within your heart. Sometimes, the heart is inclined to one more than the other, and you have no control over this. The command of equality and fairness is in regard to the outer behaviour, treatment, and attitude. We also have to make sure we don't break any law of the land we live in.

WISDOMS BEHIND POLYGAMY

There is a great deal of wisdom behind the concept of polygamy and many books have been written in this regard. If one pays careful thought to this matter, the wisdom is self-evident, as is the fact that men are naturally polygamous and women naturally monogamous.

One thing that is important to mention here is that one should never think that polygamy is bad as this could affect their *Īmān*. If you think that Allāh's ﷻ command is wrong or bad, then your faith is at risk. You can tell your husband and make an agreement with him that he does not marry anyone else while he is married to you, but you

[162] Abu Dāwūd: 2133; Ibn Mājah: 2045.

[163] Qur'ān 4:129.

cannot question the validity of the allowance of polygamy within Islam.

HOW DO WOMEN DEAL WITH POLYGAMY IF THEY ARE UNHAPPY THAT THE HUSBAND HAS TAKEN A SECOND WIFE?

Ṣabr (patience) is first and foremost, as Allāh ﷻ states:

يٰاَيُّهَا الَّذِيْنَ اٰمَنُوا اسْتَعِيْنُوْا بِالصَّبْرِ وَالصَّلٰوةِ ؕ اِنَّ اللّٰهَ مَعَ الصّٰبِرِيْنَ ۝

O you who believe, seek help through patience and prayer.
Surely, Allāh is with those who are patient. [164]

Even the wives of the Beloved Prophet ﷺ sometimes felt the pressure of being co-wives, but they said to themselves it is the right of Rasūlullāh ﷺ and consoled themselves. Think of the sacrifice and courage of the Mother of the Believers, Lady Sawdah bint Zam'ạ رضي الله عنها, who fearing that the Beloved Prophet ﷺ would divorce her, gave up her share of time and gifted it to 'Ā'ishah رضي الله عنها in order to remain married to him:

قَالَتْ عَائِشَةُ يَا ابْنَ أُخْتِي كَانَ رَسُولُ اللهِ ﷺ لاَ يُفَضِّلُ بَعْضَنَا عَلَى بَعْضٍ فِي الْقَسْمِ مِنْ مُكْثِهِ عِنْدَنَا وَكَانَ قَلَّ يَوْمٌ إِلاَّ وَهُوَ يَطُوفُ عَلَيْنَا جَمِيعًا فَيَدْنُو مِنْ كُلِّ امْرَأَةٍ مِنْ غَيْرِ مَسِيسٍ حَتَّى يَبْلُغَ إِلَى الَّتِي هُوَ يَوْمُهَا فَيَبِيتُ عِنْدَهَا وَلَقَدْ قَالَتْ سَوْدَةُ بِنْتُ زَمْعَةَ حِينَ أَسَنَّتْ وَفَرِقَتْ أَنْ يُفَارِقَهَا رَسُولُ اللهِ صلى الله عليه وسلم يَا رَسُولَ اللهِ يَوْمِي لِعَائِشَةَ . فَقَبِلَ ذَلِكَ رَسُولُ اللهِ

[164] Qur'ān 2:153.

ﷺ مِنْهَا قَالَتْ نَقُولُ فِي ذَلِكَ أَنْزَلَ الله تَعَالَى وَفِي أَشْبَاهِهَا أُرَاهُ قَالَ { وَإِنِ امْرَأَةٌ خَافَتْ مِنْ بَعْلِهَا نُشُوزًا }

'Ā'ishah said: O my nephew, the Messenger of Allāh (ﷺ) did not prefer one of us to the other in respect of his division of the time of his staying with us. It was very rare that he did not visit us any day (i.e. he visited all of us every day). He would come near each of his wives without having intercourse with her until he reached the one who had her day and passed his night with her. When Sawdah daughter of Zam'ạ became old and feared that the Messenger of Allāh (ﷺ) would divorce her, she said: Messenger of Allāh! I give to 'Ā'ishah the day you visit me. The Messenger of Allāh (ﷺ) accepted it from her. She said: We think that Allāh, the Exalted, revealed about this or similar matter of other women in the Qur'ānic verse: 'If a wife fears desertion on her husband's part then there is no harm upon them if they were to reconcile among them, and reconciliation is better.' [165]

HAVING CHILDREN

This is a primary reason for marriage and a command from Allāh ﷻ, and also the wish of the Beloved Prophet ﷺ. Allāh ﷻ states:

فَالْـٰٔنَ بَاشِرُوْهُنَّ وَابْتَغُوْا مَا كَتَبَ اللهُ لَكُمْ ۝

So now you can have sexual intimacy with them and seek what Allāh has destined for you. [166]

The Beloved Messenger ﷺ states:

تَزَوَّجُوا الْوَدُودَ الْوَلُودَ فَإِنِّي مُكَاثِرٌ بِكُمُ الأُمَمَ.

Marry women who are loving and (prolific in) childbearing, for I shall outnumber the other nations by you. [167]

---

[165] Abū Dāwūd: 2135; Ibn Mājah: 2048.

[166] Qur'ān 2:187.

[167] Abū Dāwūd: 2050.

Just as we feel pride upon seeing our whole family gathered, with all our children, grandchildren, or even great grandchildren present, so too will the prophets and messengers on the Day of Judgement when they look upon their nations. It will be a source of great pride for Rasūlullāh ﷺ to see the vast numbers of his *Ummah*, so we should try to have as many children as we can.

Those who are struggling to have children should pray the following *du'ās* after every *Fardh ṣalāh*:

رَبَّنَا هَبْ لَنَا مِنْ اَزْوَاجِنَا وَذُرِّيّٰتِنَا قُرَّةَ اَعْيُنٍ وَّاجْعَلْنَا لِلْمُتَّقِيْنَ اِمَامًا ۝

Our Lord, Give us, from our spouses and our children, comfort of eyes, and make us Imāms [guides] of the God-Fearing. [168]

رَبِّ لَا تَذَرْنِىْ فَرْدًا وَّاَنْتَ خَيْرُ الْوٰرِثِيْنَ ۝

My Lord, do not leave me single, and You are the best of inheritors. [169]

THE CHILDLESS COUPLE AND IVF TREATMENT

If you don't have children, try your best through medical means to help your situation. Go to the doctors and try medication, as well as alternative medication such as homeopathic treatments. Something will work *Inshāllāh* somehow, somewhere, sometime. If it does not, then we come to the matter of IVF treatment.

You cannot jump straight to IVF treatment at the beginning of your marriage. However, if you have been trying for many years with no success and nothing seems to be working, *then* you can consider IVF treatment. Go to a *mufti* who can assess your individual case and situation, and if he will permit you then *Inshāllāh* go forward with IVF. Within this treatment, you have to be careful and cautious to make sure that only the semen of the husband is used for the treatment

[168] Qur'ān 25:74.

[169] Qur'ān 21:89.

rather than it being mixed with anything else. There are certain clinics who mix things as well. If another person's semen is mixed in as well, then the lineage of the child born from this procedure comes into doubt. So, one should make sure that only the husband's semen is fortified and used and not mixed with anyone else's, so that the lineage can remain certain.

To conclude this matter, IVF can be allowed in certain situations if the doctor suggests that it will be beneficial. It must be remembered that IVF does not always work the first time, and sometimes you may have to take the treatment three or four times to be successful. There is the case of a friend of mine who underwent the treatment three times without success. *Alhamdulillāh*, on the fourth attempt his wife became pregnant, and gave birth to twins.

If after trying everything, a couple remain childless, they should take solace from the case of many around the world who have no children. Apart from Hadhrat Khadījah ؉, the other wives never had any children from *Rasūlullāh* ﷺ. Hadhrat 'Ā'ishah ؉ became a widow before reaching the age of 20. She spent 48 years of her life as a widow. She never complained of not having any children.

Whilst we should try our best, leave no stones unturned, we should also be content with whatever Allāh ﷻ decided for us.

ADOPTION & FOSTERING

There are two separate issues here: one is fostering and the other is adoption. With fostering, there is no problem as the child keeps their name and familial identity. However, with adoption, as the child is completely taken in by a new family with a new surname being given etc., it is necessary that when they are old enough, they are told of their true and identity, who they are and where they came from. If you do not and you hide the truth of their origins, this is very wrong. Allāh ﷻ states:

اُدْعُوْهُمْ لِاٰبَآئِهِمْ هُوَ أَقْسَطُ عِنْدَ اللهِ ج فَاِنْ لَّمْ تَعْلَمُوْٓا آبَاءَهُمْ فَاِخْوَانُكُمْ فِى الدِّيْنِ وَمَوَالِيكُمْ ط وَلَيْسَ عَلَيْكُمْ جُنَاحٌ فِيمَآ اَخْطَاْتُمْ بِهٖ لا وَلٰكِنْ مَّا تَعَمَّدَتْ قُلُوبُكُمْ ط وَكَانَ اللهُ غَفُورًا رَّحِيمًا ۝

Call them by (the name of) their (real) fathers; It is more equitable in the sight of Allāh. And if you do not know their fathers, then they are your brothers in faith and your friends. There is no sin on you in the mistake you make, but in that which you do with intention of your heart; and Allāh is Most-Forgiving, Very-Merciful. [170]

Fostering keeps their identity and can also be highly rewarding. This is because the child is like a *yatīm* [an orphan]. The virtues of looking after a *yatīm* can be applied here as well. Muslims should come forward and look after children who are abandoned for whatever reason.

One *ḥadīth* states:

خَيْرُ بَيْتٍ فِي الْمُسْلِمِينَ بَيْتٌ فِيهِ يَتِيمٌ يُحْسَنُ إِلَيْهِ،
وَشَرُّ بَيْتٍ فِي الْمُسْلِمِينَ بَيْتٌ فِيهِ يَتِيمٌ يُسَاءُ إِلَيْهِ -

"The best house among the households of Muslims is the one in which there is an orphan who is treated well. And the worst house among the Muslims is the house in which there is an orphan who is treated badly." [171]

One *Ṣaḥābī* complained of hard-heartedness. He was instructed to stroke the head of an orphan, visit the sick, and participate in funerals. This softened his heart. [172]

One *ḥadīth* says:

أَنَا وَكَافِلُ الْيَتِيمِ فِي الْجَنَّةِ كَهَاتَيْنِ(يُشِيرُ بِإِصْبَعَيْهِ) -

---

[170] Qur'ān 33:5,

[171] Ibn Mājah: 3679.

[172] Mishkāt.

"I, and the one who looks after an orphan will be like this in Paradise." (And he gestured by joining the index finger with the middle one). [173]

Ḥāfiz ibn Ḥajar narrates here that, 'Every Muslim should strive to take good care of an orphan so he can be with *Rasūlullāh* ﷺ in *Jannah*.'

Another *ḥadīth* says: 'Whoever strokes the head of an orphan due to tenderness, will get the reward equal to every hair that is covered by his hand.'[174]

PREGNANCY

During pregnancy, women go through lots of difficulties. And for each of these difficulties they pass through, they gain tremendous *thawāb* (reward). Our *Dīn* is amazing, even if you are pricked by a thorn it is a means of having your sins forgiven. It is narrated in the *aḥādīth* that:

مَا مِنْ مُصِيبَةٍ تُصِيبُ الْمُسْلِمَ إِلاَّ كَفَّرَ اللهُ بِهَا عَنْهُ، حَتَّى الشَّوْكَةِ يُشَاكُهَا.

No calamity befalls a Muslim but that Allāh expiates some of his sins because of it, even though it were the prick he receives from a thorn. [175]

قَارِبُوا وَسَدِّدُوا فَفِي كُلِّ مَا يُصَابُ بِهِ الْمُسْلِمُ
كَفَّارَةٌ حَتَّى النَّكْبَةِ يُنْكَبُهَا أَوِ الشَّوْكَةِ يُشَاكُهَا.

Be moderate and stand firm in trouble that falls to the lot of a Muslim (as that) is an expiation for him; even stumbling on the path or the pricking of a thorn (are an expiation for him). [176]

Headaches, fever, and morning sickness may be inconveniences and troubles in the short term, but they are a means of having sins forgiven. It is narrated in the *aḥādīth* that:

---

[173] Bukhārī: 6005.

[174] Ahmed.

[175] Bukhārī: 5640, 5641, 5642, 5648; Muslim: 2572e, 2572f, 2572g; Tirmidhī: 965.

[176] Muslim: 2574; Tirmidhī: 3312.

مَا مِنْ مُسْلِمٍ يُصِيبُهُ أَذًى مَرَضٌ فَمَا سِوَاهُ إِلاَّ حَطَّ اللهُ سَيِّئَاتِهِ كَمَا تَحُطُّ الشَّجَرَةُ وَرَقَهَا.

No Muslim is afflicted with hurt caused by disease or some other inconvenience, but that Allāh will remove his sins as a tree sheds its leaves [in autumn]. [177]

لاَ تَسُبِّي الْحُمَّى فَإِنَّهَا تُذْهِبُ خَطَايَا بَنِي آدَمَ كَمَا يُذْهِبُ الْكِيرُ خَبَثَ الْحَدِيدِ.

'Do not curse fever, for it expiates the sin of the children of Adam just as furnace removes the filth from iron.[178]

So any form of discomfort or inconvenience is actually good for a Muslim, as it expiates their sins and becomes a means for reward. When women go through difficulties during pregnancy, such as morning sickness, stomach aches, headaches, and sleepless nights, it is a means of having sins forgiven and ranks raised in Allāh's eyes and so should not become despondent and should bear it with patience.

DESIRE FOR A BOY OR GIRL

There is no harm in having such desire or praying for such. However, you should not consider one as inferior to the other. Whatever Allāh ﷻ blesses you with, you should be content with it.

SUPPLICATIONS TO MAKE PREGNANCY EASY

During your pregnancy, you should recite *Sūrah Maryam* every day as it is good for the child as well as for an easy pregnancy and childbirth. It should be recited every day, after which you should make *duā* that Allāh ﷻ makes your pregnancy easy.

[177] Bukhārī: 5647, 5661, 5667.

[178] Muslim: 2575; Tirmidhī: 3259; Ibn Mājah: 3598.

For getting married, our *Hadhrat* mentions reciting *Sūrah Yūsuf* every day and for pregnancy we have the recital of *Sūrah Maryam.*

WHAT DOES ISLAM SAY ABOUT NATURAL BIRTHS VS CAESAREAN BIRTHS ?

You should try to opt for a natural birth as much as it is viable, and a caesarean should only be resorted to if a life is at risk.

There was once a case about which I asked my *Shaykh* regarding a woman having a caesarean. *Hadhrat* said that I should tell her to inform the doctor that she would be prepared to die during childbirth but would not have an operation done. She was strong and steadfast upon it, even though the doctor said that she has had a caesarean birth before so would have to have it again. The doctors gave her a fourteen day limit and the next Monday they would induce her. She tried every herbal medicine and asked for some *duās* which to read. There is one *hadīth* in *Tuḥfā-e-Ḥuffāẓ* in which it is mentioned that when the Lady Fāṭima ﵂ was pregnant and about to give birth, *Rasūlullāh* ﷺ said to Asmā bint Umais ﵂ to tell her to recite the following verses and blow on her:

اَللّٰهُ لَآ اِلٰهَ اِلَّا هُوَ الْحَيُّ الْقَيُّوْمُ ج لَا تَاْخُذُهٗ سِنَةٌ وَّلَا نَوْمٌ ط لَهٗ مَا فِي السَّمٰوٰتِ
وَمَا فِي الْاَرْضِ ط مَنْ ذَا الَّذِيْ يَشْفَعُ عِنْدَهٗٓ اِلَّا بِاِذْنِهٖ ط يَعْلَمُ مَا بَيْنَ اَيْدِيْهِمْ
وَمَا خَلْفَهُمْ ج وَلَا يُحِيْطُوْنَ بِشَيْءٍ مِّنْ عِلْمِهٖٓ اِلَّا بِمَا شَآءَ ج وَسِعَ كُرْسِيُّهُ
السَّمٰوٰتِ وَالْاَرْضَ ج وَلَا يَئُوْدُهٗ حِفْظُهُمَا ج وَهُوَ الْعَلِيُّ الْعَظِيْمُ ۝

Allāh: There is no god but He, the Living, the All-Sustaining. Neither dozing overtakes Him nor sleep. To Him belongs all that is in the heavens and all that is on the earth. Who can intercede with Him except after His permission? He knows what is before them and what is behind them; while they encompass nothing of His knowledge, except what He wills. His Kursiyy (Throne) extends to the Heavens and to the Earth, and it does not weary Him to look after them. He is the All-High, the Supreme. [179]

إِنَّ رَبَّكُمُ اللّٰهُ الَّذِيْ خَلَقَ السَّمٰوٰتِ وَالْاَرْضَ فِيْ سِتَّةِ اَيَّامٍ ثُمَّ اسْتَوٰى عَلَى الْعَرْشِ قف يُغْشِى الَّيْلَ النَّهَارَ يَطْلُبُهٗ حَثِيْثًا وَّالشَّمْسَ وَالْقَمَرَ وَالنُّجُوْمَ مُسَخَّرٰتٍ م بِاَمْرِهٖ ط اَلَا لَهُ الْخَلْقُ وَالْاَمْرُ ط تَبٰرَكَ اللّٰهُ رَبُّ الْعٰلَمِيْنَ ○

"Surely, your Lord is Allāh who created the heavens and the earth in six days, then He positioned himself on the Throne. He covers the day with the night that pursues it swiftly. (He created) the sun and the moon and the stars, subjugated to His command. Lo! To Him alone belong the creation and the command. Glorious is Allāh, the Lord of all the worlds." [180]

As well as these verses, I told her to also constantly recite:

ثُمَّ السَّبِيْلَ يَسَّرَهٗ ۔

Then He (Allāh) made the way easy for him. [181]

And so as childbirth approached she made constant *dhikr* of this verse as well. The nurses told her that her heart rate at the time of childbirth was the calmest that they had ever seen. This was because, during those most difficult moments, her heart and mind remained attached to Allāh ﷻ.

MISCARRIAGE

If a miscarriage occurs, then again one should do *Ṣabr* on its passing as this child will be a means of great reward for you and will save you on the Day of Resurrection. It is narrated in the *aḥādīth* that:

إِنَّ السِّقْطَ لَيُرَاغِمُ رَبَّهُ إِذَا أَدْخَلَ أَبَوَيْهِ النَّارَ . فَيُقَالُ أَيُّهَا السِّقْطُ

---

[179] Qur'ān 2:255.

[180] Qur'ān 7:54.

[181] Qur'ān 80:20.

الْمُرَاغِمُ رَبَّهُ أَدْخِلْ أَبَوَيْكَ الْجَنَّةَ . فَيَجُرُّهُمَا بِسَرَرِهِ حَتَّى يُدْخِلَهُمَا الْجَنَّةَ .

The miscarried foetus will plead with his Lord if his parents are admitted to Hell. It will be said, 'O foetus who pleads with your Lord! Admit your parents to Paradise.' So he will drag them out with his umbilical cord until he admits them to Paradise. [182]

وَالَّذِي نَفْسِي بِيَدِهِ إِنَّ السِّقْطَ لَيَجُرُّ أُمَّهُ بِسَرَرِهِ إِلَى الْجَنَّةِ إِذَا احْتَسَبَتْهُ .

By the One in Whose Hand is my soul! The miscarried foetus will drag his mother by his umbilical cord to Paradise, if she (was patient and) sought reward (for her loss). [183]

The miscarried child, if you are patient, is a great reward for you. One of my friends' spouse was pregnant. After many scans and checks, the doctor informed them that the child had Down syndrome and was in a very weak condition and would most likely not survive past two weeks after birth. He suggested to them that they should opt for an abortion. My friend came to me for advice, so I asked him, 'How strong is your wife.' 'My wife is even stronger than me,' he replied. So I told him not to give up so much *thawāb* that would be coming their way: the *thawāb* of pregnancy, followed by the *thawāb* of childbirth, followed by the *thawāb* of those two weeks of life, followed by the *thawāb* of remaining patient upon the death of their child. They agreed to this and went ahead with the birth. At a later date, he told me that in those two weeks he had gained many memories which he would cherish for the rest of his life. Even in the most difficult moments, be patient and hope for the reward of Allāh ﷻ.

UNRULY CHILDREN

If a couple do have children and they are badly behaved, they should try their best to teach them good *Akhlāq*. There are certain *duās* which parents can make for them:

[182] Ibn Mājah: 1676.

[183] Ibn Mājah: 1677.

رَبَّنَا هَبْ لَنَا مِنْ أَزْوَاجِنَا وَذُرِّيَّاتِنَا قُرَّةَ أَعْيُنٍ وَاجْعَلْنَا لِلْمُتَّقِينَ إِمَامًا ۝

'O our Rabb! Grant us the coolness of our eyes from our spouses and children and make us Imāms of the pious.' [184]

رَبِّ هَبْ لِي مِنَ الصَّالِحِينَ ۝

O my Rabb! Grant me a son from among the pious. [185]

رَبِّ هَبْ لِي مِنْ لَّدُنْكَ ذُرِّيَّةً طَيِّبَةً ج إِنَّكَ سَمِيعُ الدُّعَاءِ ۝

My Rabb, grant me pious children from Yourself. Without doubt You hear all prayers.[186]

Read the above *duās* after every *Fardh ṣalāh* and make special *duā* for the misbehaving child.

TEN GOLDEN ADVICES [187]

أما الأولى:

أي بني : إنّك لن تنال السعادة في بيتك إلا بعشر

خصال تمنحها لزوجك فاحفظها عني واحرص عليها.

Dear son, you will not attain good fortune in your home except by 10 characteristics which you show to your wife, so remember them and be enthusiastic in acting upon them.

---

[184] Qur'ān 25:74.

[185] Qur'ān 37:100.

[186] Qur'ān 3:38.

[187] This was received as Īmām Ahmed's ﵀ advice upon his son but upon investigation it turned out to be related to Shaykh Abdul Lateef Albareejawi ﵀ who related this advice to his son. Allāh knows best.

والثانية:

فإنّ النّساء يحببن الدلال ويحببن التصريح بالحب، فلا تبخل على زوجتك بذلك، فإن بخلت جعلت بينك وبينها حجابًا من الجفوة ونقصًا في المودة.

As for the first two; women like attention and they like to be told clearly that they are loved. So don't be stingy in expressing your love for your wife. If you become limited in expressing your love, you will create a barrier of harshness between you and her, and there will be a decrease in affection.

وأما الثالثة:

فإنّ النّساء يكرهنَ الرجل الشديدَ الحازم ويستخدمن الرجل الضعيف اللين، فاجعل لكل صفة مكانها، فإنّه أدعى للحب وأجلب للطمأنينة.

Ladies hate a strict, overcautious man, yet they seek to use the soft vulnerable one. So use each quality appropriately. This will be more appealing for love and it will bring you peace of mind.

وأما الرابعة:

فإنّ النساء يُحببن من الزوج ما يحب الزوج منهنّ من طيب الكلام وحسن المنظر ونظافة الثياب وطيب الرائحة، فكن في كل أحوالك كذلك.

Ladies like from their husbands what their husbands like from them, i.e. kind words, good looks, clean clothes and a pleasant odour. Therefore, always remain in that state.

أما الخامسة:

فإنّ البيت مملكة الأنثى وفيه تشعر أنّها متربعة على عرشها وأنها سيدة فيه، فإيّاك أن تهدم هذه المملكة التي تعيشها، وإياك أن تحاول أن تزيحها عن عرشها هذا، فإنّك إن فعلت نازعتها ملكها، وليس لملكٍ أشدّ عداوةً ممن ينازعه ملكه وإن أظهر له غير ذلك.

Indeed, the house is under the sovereignty of the woman. While she remains therein, she feels that she is sitting upon her throne, and that she is the chief of the house. Stay clear of destroying this kingdom of hers and do not ever attempt to dethrone her, otherwise you will be trying to snatch her sovereignty. A king gets most angry at he who tries to strip him of his authority, even if he portrays to show something else.

أما السادسة:

فإنّ المرأة تحب أن تكسب زوجها ولا تخسر أهلها، فإيّاك أن تجعل نفسك مع أهلها في ميزان واحد، فإمّا أنت وإمّا أهلها، فهي وإن اختارتك على أهلها فإنّها ستبقى في كمدٍ تُنقل عَدْواه إلى حياتك اليومية.

A woman wants to love her husband, but at the same time she does not want to lose her family. So do not put yourself and her family in the same scale, because then her choice will be down to either you or her family. And even if she does choose you over her family, she will remain in anxiety, which will then turn into hatred towards you in your daily life.

والسابعة:

إنّ المرأة خُلِقت مِن ضِلعٍ أعوج وهذا سرّ الجمال فيها، وسرُّ الجذب إليها

وليس هذا عيبًا فيها "فالحاجب زيّنه العِوَجُ"، فلا تحمل عليها إن هي أخطأت حملةً لا هوادة فيها تحاول تقييم المعوج فتكسرها وكسرها طلاقها، ولا تتركها إن هي أخطأت حتى يزداد اعوجاجها وتتقوقع على نفسها فلا تلين لك بعد ذلك ولا تسمع إليك، ولكن كن دائما معها بين بين.

Surely woman has been created from a curved rib, and this is the secret of her beauty, and the secret of the attraction towards her. And this is no defect in her, because 'the eyebrows look beautiful due to them being curved'. So if she errs, do not rebuke her in a manner in which there is no gentleness, attempting to straighten her; otherwise you will simply break her and her breaking, is her divorce. At the same time do not let her off upon that mistake, otherwise her crookedness will increase, and she will become arrogant with her ego. Thereafter, she will never soften for you and she won't listen to you, so stay in between the two.

أما الثامنة:

فإنّ النّساء جُبلن على كُفر العشير وجُحدان المعروف، فإن أحسنت لإحداهنّ دهرًا ثم أسأت إليها مرة قالت: ما وجدت منك خيرًا قط، فلا يحملنّك هذا الخلق على أن تكرهها وتنفر منها، فإنّك إن كرهت منها هذا الخلق رضيت منها غيره.

It is in the women's nature to be ungrateful towards their husbands and to deny favours. If you were to be nice to her for her whole life but you grieved her once, she will say, "I have never seen any good from you". So don't let this attitude of her make you dislike her or to run away from her. If you dislike this feature of hers, you will be pleased with some other good habits within her, so create a balance.

أما التاسعة:

فإنّ المرأة تمر بحالات من الضعف الجسدي والتعب النفسي، حتى إنّ الله سبحانه وتعالى أسقط عنها مجموعةً من الفرائض التي افترضها في هذه الحالات؛ فقد أسقط عنها الصلاة نهائيًا في هذه الحالات وأنسأ لها الصيام خلالهما حتى تعود صحتها ويعتدل مزاجُها، فكن معها في هذه الأحوال ربانيًا، كما خفف الله سبحانه وتعالى عنها فرائضه أن تخفف عنها طلباتك وأوامرك.

Surely there are times when a woman goes through some conditions of bodily weakness and fatigue of the mind. Such that Allāh has relieved her of some of her compulsory worships during that period; Allāh has totally pardoned her from praying, and has postponed the days of fasting for her within this break to a later date until she regains her health and becomes normal in her temperament once more. Thus, during these days, treat her in a godly manner. Just as Allāh has relieved her of the duties, you should also lessen your demands and instructions from her during those days.

أما العاشرة:

فاعلم أنّ المرأة أسيرة عندك، فارحم أسرها وتجاوز عن ضعفها، تكن لك خير متاع وخير شريك.

Last but not least, know that a woman is like a captive with you. Therefore, have mercy upon her.

THE KEY TO A SUCCESSFUL MARRIAGE

There is a book which explains how to avoid arguments and disputes and be a good lifelong partner. It is called, *Men are from Mars and Women are from Venus* and is a very good book on this subject which everyone should read.

Some really good advice for a successful marriage was given at a *nikāḥ* by one of my friends. I edited it and have added a few things.

He said, 'There are certain 'T's needed for a marriage to be successful and prosperous.' They are as follows:

T for *Taqwā*: *Taqwā* is the foundation of a successful marriage. Both partners should adopt a life of *taqwā*. Be constantly aware of Allāh ﷻ. Fulfil His rights and He will look after both of you. The Fear of Allāh ﷻ allows both parties to live in harmony. Maybe this is why the three verses *Rasūlullāh* ﷺ recited in the *Khuṭbah* of *Nikāḥ* are all regarding *taqwā*. Most *Imāms* read the same three verses.

T is for Trust: Trust one another. *Rasūlullāh* ﷺ was the most trustworthy person to have set foot on the face of this earth. He trusted his wives. He would defend them against any accusations. They trusted him at all times. Follow their *Sunnah*. Don't lose trust in your partner and don't allow any room for doubts. Don't let *Shayṭān* creep in with whispers.

T is for Tongue: Control your tongue when speaking to your spouse. Don't speak rudely. Be soft and gentle. Gentleness is amazing magic, it works wonders. One *ḥadīth* says:

عَلَيْكِ بِالرِّفْقِ فَإِنَّ الرِّفْقَ لَا يَكُونُ فِي شَيْءٍ إِلَّا زَانَهُ وَلَا يُنْزَعُ مِنْ شَيْءٍ إِلَّا شَانَهُ.

'Be gentle. Gentleness does not prevail in anything except it beautifies it, whereas harshness does not come into something without making it ugly.' [188]

Maybe this is why in one of the verses in the *Khuṭbah* of *Nikāḥ*, Allāh ﷻ says:

وَقُوْلُوا قَوْلًا سَدِيْدًا ۝

'. . . And speak the right words . . .' [189]

Always think before you speak. One wise Urdu quote says:

---

[188] Musnad Aḥmad: 24417.

[189] Qur'ān 33: 70.

عقلمند سوچ کر بولتا ہے اور بے وقوف بول کر سوچتا ہے ۔

"A wise person thinks before he speaks, whereas a fool speaks first, and then thinks" (what did I just say?)

An elderly lady was once asked about the secret of her successful marriage. She replied: 'Whenever he got angry, I would just keep quiet and listen to him. I knew that my husband had had a hard day at work. I would then go into the kitchen and give him time to calm down. I would bring him a nice cup of tea. He would ask me if I was angry with him, and I would say, 'No I am not angry with you.' She was asked, 'Would you be serious?' She replied, 'Of course I would be serious, I'm not a hypocrite.' He would then apologise and be very kind and show affection. If I ever got angry for some reason, he would stay calm and keep things under control.

T is for Talk: Communicate with your spouse regularly. Let them know your feelings. These days there is a lack of communication everywhere. People are so busy with their hobbies or with their mobile phones, that they don't have time for anyone. So make sure you talk to one another.

T is for Time: Take time out to spend with your partner, and realise that once you get married, your lifestyle has to change. You might have to compromise with your nights out with friends, and with your sports, etc.

T is for Tea: Make sure you have tea together, and that you eat and drink together at the same time as this creates love between two people. When sitting down for eating, you can share your feelings, ask questions, make plans etc.

T is for Tolerance: Nobody is perfect, so look at the good qualities in your partner and tolerate the bad ones with patience. If they inform you of anything they dislike, ponder over it, and if they are right, rectify it. Try not to be stubborn.

T is for Technology: Technology can make or break a relationship. Don't allow it to become the third person in your relationship. Avoid wasting time on social media. One newlywed couple went abroad for their honeymoon. The girl was constantly engaged on her phone. The young man tried to reason with her, but she said, 'I have so many messages congratulating me, I have to reply to all of them, I can't be rude to my friends.' They had a fight and ended up separating.

T is for Trouble Makers: Don't allow the rumours and comments of others to spoil the harmony between you and your partner. There are plenty of jealous people out there who don't want to see you happy. They will make every attempt to cause a rift between you. Don't listen to them.

T is for Tahajjud: Wake up in the night for *Tahajjud* and even pray together and encourage each other to do good deeds. One *ḥadīth* states: 'May Allāh have mercy on that man who woke up for *Tahajjud* and awakened his wife. If she didn't wake up, he sprinkled some water on her, so she woke up, and they both prayed two *rak'ạh.* May Allāh have mercy on that woman who woke up at night and awakened her husband. If he didn't wake up, she sprinkled some water on him, and he woke up, and they both prayed two *rak'ạh.*

Finally, *T is for Tawfīq:* We make *duā* that Allāh ﷻ gives us all the *tawfīq* to implement these advices into our own lives and to pass them on, so others can also benefit *Inshāllāh. Āmīn.*

May Allāh ﷻ accept this humble effort and make it beneficial for those who are looking to get married as well as for those who are already married. *Āmīn.*